ERRATA.

Readers of the Proceedings and Report of the Board of Civil Engineers, convened in St. Louis in August, 1867, etc., etc., will please make the following corrections:

On page 55, for $(W_3—W)=E$, read $(W_3—W_1)=E$.
" " 55, for $(W_2—W)=T$, read $(W_2—W_1)=T$.
" " 59, for h i 1,886,513¾, read h i 1,086.513¾.
" " 59, for o p 1,503,551¾, read o p 1,665,551¾.
" " 59, for p p′ 1,521,178¾, read p p′ 1,727,096¾.
" " 98, 26 lines from top, for increase, read income.

PROCEEDINGS AND REPORT

OF THE

BOARD OF CIVIL ENGINEERS

CONVENED AT ST. LOUIS, IN AUGUST, 1867,

TO CONSIDER THE SUBJECT OF THE CONSTRUCTION OF A

RAIL AND HIGHWAY BRIDGE

ACROSS THE MISSISSIPPI RIVER AT ST. LOUIS.

ST. LOUIS:
GEORGE KNAPP & CO., PRINTERS AND BINDERS.
1867.

PROCEEDINGS

OF

BRIDGE CONVENTION.

St. Louis, *August* 21, 1867.

A meeting of engineers and gentlemen interested in bridging the Mississippi river at St. Louis, was held this day at room No. 6, of the Southern Hotel.

Col. Anderson called the meeting to order, and on his motion, seconded by General Smith, Wm. J. McAlpine, of New York, was unanimously elected President, and T. McKissock, Chief Engineer Pacific R.R. of Missouri, Secretary of the Convention.

Mr. McAlpine, upon taking the chair, made the following remarks:

"*Gentlemen*—For the honor which you have conferred in calling upon me to preside over your deliberations, I beg to return to you my profound thanks.

Believing, as I do, that the profession to which we belong is deserving of the highest rank in the scale of social progress, and observing among the gentlemen here assembled those of the highest standing, increases my obligation for the compliment which you have paid me. I presume that it is in part due to the fact that I am almost the oldest practising civil engineer in the United States; but to whatever cause I am indebted for your kindness, I have again to thank you, and assure you that I will endeavor to discharge the duties of your presiding officer so as to carry out your wishes, and accomplish the results aimed at in calling us together.

The problem which is presented to us is not only one of the most interesting ones before the profession, but also involves other considerations of the highest commercial importance.

In preparing plans for bridging the Mississippi, we must give due attention to the relative importance of the navigation of the river, and of the traffic which the bridge is to accommodate. The former is one of the most important inland water channels in the world, and the latter is to form a connecting link in one of the most important lines of land transport across the continent.

We are now nearly in the geographical centre of the nation, and when it becomes thoroughly reunited, as before, and recovers from the disastrous effects of war, this point will also become one of, and perhaps the largest, of the two internal commercial centres on the northern continent.

At this place now concentrates, as nowhere else on the Mississippi, the great trunk lines of railways extending westward from a range of the Atlantic coast between Boston and Baltimore. From this point radiate as many lines of railways towards the farther interior, and to the Pacific. On the other hand, we stand at the head of navigation, by the class of vessels best suited to the lower river, and at the foot of the navigation by vessels best suited for the upper river, and its not less important navigable tributaries.

The fortunate concurrence of these termini to these important lines of water transport, at the same place as the central lines of land traffic, indicates this as one of those points where the magnitude of the land transport can demand, as a commercial question, some abridgement of the water rights.

Heretofore, the traditional importance of the navigable water-lines has controlled legislation, and the legal tribunals, almost wholly in their favor. The last third of a century has developed a traffic over the land lines of transport of such importance, that modern legislation and legal decisions have been compelled to concede the right to carry railroads across the navigable waters; and although this legislation has not yet risen to the correct view of the question (namely, that they should each yield and have the right of occupancy in proportion to their relative importance), yet it has made such progress that, as Sir Francis Head not long ago said in regard to the Britannia bridge, "the man of science must no longer, cap in hand, bow to the man of law."

The Federal and State laws under which the bridge at this

place is to be built, require an elevation sufficient to allow steamers, with their unnecessarily high chimneys, to pass at the highest stage of water, and with spans of unnecessary width for the navigation. "The men of science" must thus far "bow to the men of law," and it is this necessity which has compelled the officers of the Bridge Company to bring to the consideration of these grave subjects such an array of the "men of science."

Although we have been convened at the request of one of the rival companies, yet we are to consider all of the questions bearing on this subject, without reference to any particular plan or company. We have among our numbers the pioneer of the pneumatic pile foundations, and his eminent successor; the constructor of the caisson-built piers of the Susquehanna; the builder of the Lake Michigan tunnel; the veteran bridge-builder, who has made the longest wooden span in the country, and has now presented us with designs of those in iron, to meet even the requirements of the "men of law."

We have with us eminent representatives from our great national Polytechnic, and from our highest civil Universities—and I may venture to say, that the result of your deliberations is looked forward to with great interest by those both in and out of the profession; and that the belief is strongly entertained by the commercial, financial and professional gentlemen interested in this and similar enterprises, that your combined science and skill will develop the best method of overcoming the difficulties to be met in accomplishing this great undertaking.

Col. Anderson, Chief Engineer of the bridge, and formerly Chief Engineer U. S. Military Railroads, has submitted for your inspection and consideration various maps and sections of the river at St. Louis, and has suggested to you some of the difficulties which he apprehends may be met with in obtaining proper foundations for the piers.

General Smith will lay before you plans of his own for meeting these difficulties, and Mr. Parker, with his experience on the Susquehanna, will give you other plans for the same purpose. From Mr. Homer's long acquaintance, and close study of the river, you will ascertain its regimen, and obtain other most valuable information to guide you in your deliberations. Mr. Post will furnish plans for your consideration, to meet even the enormous spans required by the federal law, and these, and other gentlemen, will bring to the whole subject their experience and skill in similar undertakings. From such an array of engineering talent, we may expect a complete elucidation of the important questions before us.

The bed of the river is a loose sand, which changes for a considerable depth with every stage of water, in freshets and during their subsidence, scouring out channels, and making deposits. With the erection of the necessary piers of the bridge, this scouring will be increased, and make it necessary to place their foundations below such possible future action.

The rock lies at twenty-three feet below low water near the west shore, and slopes towards the east, reaching a depth of ninety feet at the last sounding, two-thirds of the way across the river, which is about two thousand feet wide.

Some of the gentlemen will present plans of foundations requiring the use of iron pneumatic piles, which strike me very favorably as meeting all of the requirements of the case—ample supporting power, facilities for rapid execution, and comparative economy.

If it shall be concluded that these piles shall in all cases be driven to the rock, the grave question arises, can life be supported in six atmospheres, at more than a hundred feet below the surface of the water? or will the knowledge and skill here present suggest some other practical plan for removing the interior sand, and perhaps trees and boulders? and then will follow the difficulty of basing and securing the piles to the rock.

When this is accomplished these piles will become columns of support, and you have to determine how much of their whole length is to be deducted for the support of the sand around them, to give the proper co-efficient of strength from the ratio of length and diameter. The question will also present itself, whether a sufficient support can be obtained from these piles without forcing them to the rock, where it lies at great depth? How much support will the area at the base afford? and can it be expanded by using a bell-mouthed shoe, or by tunnelling after it has been sunk to any given depth? Again, how much support will the exterior cohesion on the piles give?—of course calculating only for that portion below any future possible scour, unless you decide that you can keep this scour replaced by masses of rock filled in, but out of the way of vessels which may pass close to the piers.

Will these rocks silt up and give the same resistance and cohesion as the sand does below them?

What will be the rate of corrosion of the iron piles under water, and can that corrosion be lessened or prevented?

With what material shall these piles be filled?

How shall they be capped and spanned to enable them to carry the enormous weight of the masonry and superstructure? or shall the piles be extended up to the bridge seat? and can they be braced so that with their inherent stability they will resist the impact of floating ice, drift, or vessels?

You will also be presented with plans contemplating the use of an inverted caisson, connected with a direct but removable one above it. This will require dredging and probably curbing to the depth of the possible scour, the subdivision of the caisson, and the use of the pneumatic process for filling it with masonry.

Your attention will also be called to a plan for building stone piers based upon the rock, the details of which have been recently published in this city, and which will be laid before you. This published plan contemplates the use of three spans, of about five hundred feet each.

You will also be furnished with complete drawings of a bridge involving the use of two spans of three hundred and sixty-eight feet each, and four spans of two hundred and sixty-four feet each, for crossing the river with an iron bridge, and also of the approaches at its two ends.

The law requires a bridge to be constructed with one of its spans not less than five hundred feet clear opening, or with two spans of not less than three hundred and fifty feet each.

You will be called upon to consider whether the saving to be effected by the cost of foundation and piers will be equal to the increased cost of the superstructure in spans of such great length, and whether suitable materials can be procured and put together, so as to sustain their own weight and that of stationary and passing loads.

These and many other plans for the sub and superstructure will become the subject of your discussions, and from the previous study which many of you gentlemen have already given directly to this subject, and the great amount of practical experience which you combine on all of the matters that may come before you, it is very certain that you will arrive at conclusions which will enable the capitalists here and elsewhere to determine with safety whether they will invest in the undertaking.

In conclusion, I may remark that with the freedom and frankness which characterizes our profession, our discussions will furnish to each of us most valuable information, which sooner or later will become available in other works which we may have in hand, and, following our usual custom, we shall 'tell what we know and learn what we can,' and, by this mutual interchange of knowledge, and the results of our experience, increase our love and devotion to our profession, and the kind and genial feelings which we entertain towards our associates here assembled."

On motion it was "*Resolved,* That an invitation be extended to any parties having plans to suggest to attend the meeting and submit them for the consideration of the Convention."

Pursuant to the above motion, the following invitation was sent:

St. Louis, *August* 21, 1867.

Sir: A Board of Engineers and gentlemen interested in the question of crossing the Mississippi river at St. Louis by a Highway and Railroad Bridge, have met at St. Louis this morning, and on motion it was

"*Resolved,* That the gentlemen of St. Louis most interested in this question be invited to attend the meetings and unite in the discussions of the various important questions connected with this subject."

In accordance therewith, the Board respectfully invite you to meet with them at the Southern Hotel, Parlor No. 6, at your convenience.

Board will meet this evening at 8 o'clock, and to-morrow A. M. at 9 o'clock.

Respectfully yours,

WM. J. McALPINE, *President.*

T. McKissock, *Secretary.*

General Smith offered the following resolution:

Resolved, That for the purpose of facilitating the business before the Convention, the Chair be requested to appoint committees on the following subjects:

1. On the Regimen of the River and the character of its Bottom.
2. On the Foundations and Piers.
3. On the Superstructure and Approaches.
4. On the River Commerce and its Navigation.
5. On the Commerce crossing the Bridge.

The Convention then adjourned to meet at 3½ P. M.

St. Louis, *August* 21, 1867.

The Convention met pursuant to adjournment, President McAlpine in the chair, who announced the following committees:

1. On the Regimen of the River and the character of its Bottom—Messrs. Homer, Moulton, Moore.

2. On the Foundations and Piers—Messrs. Chesbrough, Smith, Parker, Fleming, C. L. McAlpine.

3. On the Superstructure and Approaches—Messrs. Post, Shoemaker, Fleming, Chanute, Blackstone.

4. On the River Commerce and its Navigation—Messrs. Moore, Homer, Churchill.

5. On the Commerce crossing the Bridge—Messrs. Blackstone, Anderson, McKissock, D. A. January, Chas. A. Tucker.

At the unanimous request of the committees, and on motions of the respective chairmen, it was

Resolved, That the President be specially added to the Committees on Foundations and on Superstructure, and *ex officio* to all the other committees.

The Convention then took a recess till 8 o'clock P. M.

The Convention met pursuant to adjournment, and having no business before it to enable the several committees to pursue their labors, adjourned until 9 A. M. of August 22d.

August 22, 1867.

The Convention having met, pursuant to adjournment, at 9 o'clock A. M., after a general interchange of views, proceeded to the steamboat tendered by Hon. Isacc H. Sturgeon, President N. M. R.R., and viewed the harbor, the various proposed points of crossing, and matters intimately connected with the proposed structure.

Upon the return from the excursion, the Convention being called to order, Gen. Smith offered the following resolution, stating that it was at the unanimous request of his committee:

Resolved, That Col. A. Anderson be added to the Committee upon Foundations and Piers. Which was adopted.

Gen. Smith presented a letter from Col. L. J. Fleming, stating that business called him away; but from Gen. Smith's personal experience in pneumatic pile foundations, and from their recent extended comparison of views on this and other subjects, he found that their opinions coincided on the important particulars, and desired his name attached to any report of the Convention which Gen. Smith would himself approve.

Upon the motion of Mr. Parker, it was

Resolved, That the Convention adjourn subject to the call of the President, whenever the committees are prepared to report.

August 27, 1867.

The President of the Convention having called a meeting pursuant to its order, reports were received from the several committees, as follows:

1. From Messrs. Homer and Moulton, on behalf of the Committee on the Regimen of the River and the character of its Bottom.

2. From Mr. C. L. McAlpine, Secretary of the Committee on Foundations and Piers.

3. From Mr. S. S. Post, chairman in behalf of the Committee on Superstructure and Approaches.

4. From Mr. Churchill, on behalf of the Committee on the River Commerce and Navigation.

5. From Mr. T. B. Blackstone, on behalf of Committee on the the Commerce which will cross the proposed Bridge.

The several reports were then read and carefully discussed, and after the usual amendments were made were finally adopted, and ordered to be embraced in the General Report of the Convention.

August 31, 1867.

The President submitted to the Convention a draft of a General Report, which consisted of a preface, a resumé of the several reports, and the full reports of the committees as amended. The Convention then proceeded to discuss this draft, and after amendment it was unanimously adopted. It was then

Resolved, That all of the members present be requested to sign the same before its publication, and that a copy be sent to each member not present, with the request that he shall affix his name thereto, and return to the President at St. Louis.

The Convention then appointed the President, Secretary, and Messrs. S. S. Post and F. A. Churchill, a Committee on Publication, who were directed to have the report printed, and to furnish each member with a copy.

WM. J. McALPINE, *President.*

T. McKissock, *Secretary.*

REPORT OF COMMITTEE

ON THE

REGIMEN OF THE RIVER

AND THE

CHARACTER OF ITS BOTTOM.

St. Louis, *August* 24, 1867.

Wm. J. McAlpine, Esq., *President Board of Engineers.*

Dear Sir: The Committee on the Regimen of the River and the Character of its Bottom have had the subject matter referred to them under consideration, and submit the following report in relation thereto. The questions submitted to the committee are such as would require long and patient investigation and great labor to answer them fully; but believing that a brief statement of facts and conclusions will answer all the purposes of the Board on the present occasion, your committee has concluded to present the results of their observations, leaving out the modes through which they were attained.

The Mississippi river, at St. Louis, at extreme low water, has a minimum width of 1,520 feet, and about 2,000 feet at extreme high water; these widths are in excess of what is required, and it would be safe to contract the low water channel to 1,200 feet, and the high water channel to 1,800 feet. Calling the city directrix (which is high water, as generally understood) zero, then low water is minus 33.81, and the extreme high water of 1844 was plus 7.58 feet, making a total rise and fall of 41.39 feet. The flood of 1851 was plus 2.80 feet, and that of 1858 was plus 3.20 feet. With these exceptions the high water has never exceeded zero. The period of flood varies from April to July, though the great floods usually occur in the latter part of June, and are caused by the melting of the northern snows, meeting the late spring rains on the lower tributaries. The coincidence of these conditions in the Mississippi and Missouri rivers caused the great floods above mentioned, especially that of 1844. At the periods of flood, the surface of the river is covered with immense rafts of drift wood, composed of large trees, logs, lumber, and other similar materials, frequently matted together, and generally occupying the main channel of the river; but often driven out of it by strong winds blowing transversely to it.

The maximum velocity of the current in the main channel, at a depth of 3 feet below the surface, varies from 4 feet per second at a stage of water minus 33.81 feet, to 12½ feet per second at a stage plus 7.58 feet. The average descent of the river surface is about six inches per mile.

In surveys covering a space of 30 miles, from the mouth of the Missouri river, 20 miles above, to Jefferson Barracks, 10 miles below this city, the width of the river, at extreme low water, is found to vary from 2,500 feet to 900 feet; and where it is more than about 1,200 feet wide, a bar exists, either in the middle or at one of the shores; and in places where the greatest width obtains, the channel is usually divided by bars in several parts. At St. Louis the bar is in the central part of the channel, a little to the east of the middle. This bar varies much in extent, in different years, depending upon the source of the flood, its duration, and the manner of its abatement. Thus, if the flood is from the Missouri river, and no flood in the Mississippi river, and the flood is of long duration, and abates with a rapid decline, the bar, under these circumstances attains its greatest development. If the flood is from the Mississippi river, and no flood in the Missouri river, and there occurs a long period when the river is of medium stage and the decline is gradual, then the bar attains its minimum development, as it becomes absorbed by the clear water of the Mississippi river; but it is always there, to some extent, and will so remain until the low water channel of the river is narrowed down to about 1,200 feet. Some seasons it is five feet above the low water surface at Biddle street, and 2½ feet below the same at Market street. Under these circumstances circuitous routes have to be pursued in crossing the river at the ferries, and under more favorable circumstances, no ill effects are observed. In some seasons, the ice grounds upon this bar, and it assists in producing an ice gorge in the harbor. The largest accumulation of ice is when the river is at a stage between minus 24 and extreme low water;

there is seldom much ice at a higher stage. The usual run of ice is in broken and detached masses, which at times cover the entire surface of the river, and finally press so closely together, that at narrow points in the river they cement together, forming a gorge, and the detached floating ice coming down lodges against the gorge, and gradually extends it up stream for many miles, leaving an open river below. Much of the floating ice coming from above doubles under the gorge, and often renders it solid from the surface to the bottom, and has caused the river to rise as much as 8 feet in a few hours. This gorged ice has been observed as thick as ten or twelve feet; the size of the masses of floating ice, under ordinary circumstances, is often as large as 50 by 150 feet, and 1 foot thick; but immediately at the point where the river breaks up, the masses of ice often move off in fields as large as 500 by 1,000 feet in area, and 12 to 14 inches thick. The movement usually commences very slow, and increases as the masses become smaller. The velocity of floating ice is less than three feet per second when the river is very full of it, and when not full, the velocity becomes nearly the same as the current upon which it floats. A heavy run of ice deadens the current, and consequently causes the river to rise in due proportion. The river is closed on an average about once in three years, and remains closed from 2½ days to 2½ months. It has been known to close early in December, and remain closed until the latter part of February. It usually closes in December, which is the period of extreme low water. The river generally closes by gorging, but it has been known to freeze directly over in one night. After freezing over, the river usually rises permanently from 6 to 8 feet, even after the immediate effects of gorging have ceased. If the gorge be very completely packed, the rapid rise in the river will often break it away, and the whole ice-floe will then pass off. Continuous cold weather, ranging as low as zero, and a low stage of the water, must be coincident in order to close the river, and even then it may not close here if a gorge has taken place a few miles above. A compact gorge, formed in this latitude in the early part of the season, will cause the river below to remain open and navigable throughout the winter, as the ice does not form usually with sufficient rapidity south of this latitude to cause a second gorge; and thus, obstructions placed in the river at this point so as to produce a gorge, would render this place continuously open to navigation from below.

The character of the deposit left in the bed of the river by floods, varies from a coarse silicious sand to a slime consisting of calcarious and alluminous matter with vegetable mould ; the former is deposited in and near the channel, and the latter on the low grounds and in abandoned channels, from the strong currents of the river, so that quicksand is not likely to be found in the immediate bed of the river, nor adjacent to it, at a lower level than low water. Clay deposits are sometimes formed, which are doubtless the result of special causes, and perhaps they are generally formed by deposits from the Upper Mississippi river. The shifting material at the bottom of the river changes 10 or 12 feet in the course of several seasons; a continuous change is going on, and each year it is various, depending upon the character of the floods, whence they originate, their magnitude and duration; changes of 30 feet in depth have occurred in a few years where abandoned channels silted up. It is a matter of speculation as to what depth below low water the current may exercise a scouring influence, but in a distance of 20 miles, partly above and partly below this city, a thorough sounding of the river was made during the low water period of 1860–61, and no greater depth was found than 30 feet, (the sounding being reduced to low water level,) under peculiar circumstances, such as a bridge pier might present, the scouring influence might extend to 40 feet in depth. It has been alleged that in the winter of 1855, a depth of 80 feet was found in the river, opposite to the foot of Bates street; but no credence can be given to the report, as the sounding made by R. E. Lee, U. S. A., in 1838, those of Clement Coote in 1843, (then city engineer,) those of the city engineer in 1861, and those made by H. Kayser at various periods, all contradict this statement. Indeed the greatest depth recorded by any one of the observers mentioned does not exceed 40 feet, and it is uncertain what was the stage of water when the greatest recorded depth was found. The circumstances under which this great depth existed were similar to those which would be produced by placing a bridge pier in the channel of the river in such a position that the main force of the current would break against it.

Four borings were made in the river in continuation of the north line of Green street: the first at a distance of 265 feet east of the west line of the wharf, where the rock was found coincident with the bed of the river at minus 56.70, or 22.89 feet below low water; the second at a point 500 feet east of the last point, where the rock was found at a depth of minus 97.46, or 63.65 feet below low water, and the water had a depth of 13.7 feet, leaving 49.95 as the thickness of the river deposit above the rock; the third was at a point 500 feet still further east, of the last point, where the rock was found at a depth of minus 123.33, or 89.52 feet below low water; here the water was 10.19 feet deep, leaving 79.33 feet as the thickness of the river deposit above the rock; the fourth was at a point 500 feet still further east where the boring was carried to a depth of minus 101.42, or 67.61 feet below low water, and then abandoned on account of the breaking up of the ice. At this point the water was 16.19 feet deep, and the river deposit was penetrated through a thickness of 51.42 feet. These borings were made early in the winter of 1866. As far as observed, the material was coarse sand with scattering pebbles, and at times a clayey discoloration of the water pumped out of the pipes for the first 20 feet in depth; below that depth an inch steel-shod rod was driven which appeared to pass through *compact materials* of apparently uniform density. It would be idle to speculate upon the precise character of this material, but it may be safely inferred that it is sufficiently consistent to uphold and sustain piles loaded with superincumbent weights, especially if well protected from the scouring influences by stone rip-rap. It may be here remarked that stone rip-rap is the best, cheapest and most simple method of protecting constructions based in the bed of the Mississippi river, or within the influence of its currents.

As an evidence that the bed rock, over which the river flows, is covered with hard materials, it may be stated that a series of borings were made in four sections, across the Missouri river, at the city of St. Charles, in the winter of 1866–7, the distance being 45 miles from St. Louis by river; they were made for the purpose of determining the foundations for a bridge over the Missouri river, on the line of the North Missouri railroad, and all in the space of ¾ of a mile, at distances transversely of 100 feet apart along each section. The boring was done with an inch iron boring-rod, pointed with steel, and driven with a light shackle-ram. The "overlay" found was common river sand, often moved by freshets, (but not to so low a depth, it is presumed, as, at this period, to reach the hard stratum,) was found to be on an average 3 feet thick, presenting a surface that sometimes broke the steel points and bent the boring-rods; but after piercing this stratum, the rod was easily forced down to the rock. Information, which at that time was regarded as reliable, went to show that a similarly hard stratum was found while boring for the foundations of a bridge over the Mississippi at Quincy, Illinois. From these coinciding facts it appears highly probable that this hard stratum at one time formed the bed of these rivers 45 miles above on the Missouri, and 160 miles above on the Mississippi. It is difficult to conjecture what it may be composed of, but it is most likely gravel packed in clay. At St. Charles, one unshod oak pile was driven to this hard stratum, but not through it, though it is believed that well shod piles may be driven through it, and there is no doubt that it would form sufficient lateral support for piling. Certainly no washing or scouring influence can disturb it, especially so if it be protected, even slightly, by a rip-rap of rock. The depth of the rock under the bed of the river is such that it is difficult to conceive how the scouring effects of the currents could ever reach so low, and yet it is manifest that the deep bed of the river has been excavated out of the rock by the action of currents of water; and if the forces which produced this be still active, may the river not again scour to an equal depth? It is not, however, possible that these forces are still active; for when the excavation was made, the level of the Gulf of Mexico extended along an arm of the sea to a great distance inland, some suppose as far as New Madrid, others as far as Baton Rouge; in either case, the water level of the river at St. Louis was much lower than at present, and it is easy to conceive that level to have been from 80 to 100 feet lower than it is now. If we were once within 500 miles of the Gulf (we are now about 1400 miles distant from it) and 366 feet above it, there must have been a continuous rise in the water level from the period when the excavating process ceased up to the present time; therefore the tendency of the river has been to cover the bed-work deeper and deeper, as the delta of the Mississippi extended out into the Gulf of Mexico, and the deep scouring of a former period is not possible to occur again. Besides this, there are indubitable evidences that a much larger volume of water once flowed through the Mississippi Valley to the Gulf than now finds an outlet in that direction. The upper lakes — Michigan and Superior — once emptied their vast surplus waters into the Illinois river. This combined with the other causes mentioned, seem to be so potent that it would be wonderful if we did not find evidences of deeper scouring in past periods than are apparent in the present. It is more than probable that remains of timber may be found to a depth of 40 or 50 feet, which will present obstacles in the sinking of foundations, but below that depth it is more than likely that the action of the elements, during the great length of time that has elapsed since their deposition, has destroyed every vestige of their organism, and they no longer exist as obstacles in the path of subaqueous excavations.

There may be a question as to the character of the rock found in the bed of the river, but all the evidences tend to prove that it is stratified limestone. The two artesian wells, sunk to a depth of 2,200 feet, and the out-crop along the Mississippi river, and Iron Mountain railroad south, and the Pacific railroad west, leave no doubt upon this subject. In long distances the average dip to the north-east is less than 1 in 100, so that the excavated bed of the river will present a shelving surface. It is not likely that boulders will be met with, as they are rare bodies in this vicinity. That the rock was reached in the borings mentioned, is evidenced by the points of the boring-rods being battered; and subsequent tests, 300 feet lower down the river, have closely identified the existence of the bed-rock in the same place—the city of St. Louis standing on limestone.

In conclusion, your committee would beg leave to express their keen sense of the inadequacy of this treatment of the great questions confided to them as an important branch of the subject before the assembled Board; but, desiring to extend their remarks no further than is deemed necessary to form a basis of action for the other more important committees, we close with the sincere hope that your clear understanding of the subject will supply all our omissions, and that our brief remarks may thus serve the purposes intended.

Very respectfully, your obedient servants,

(Signed,) TRUMAN J. HOMER,
(Signed,) J. B. MOULTON.

MINUTES

OF THE

PROCEEDINGS AND DISCUSSIONS

OF THE

COMMITTEE ON FOUNDATIONS AND PIERS.

A Board of Civil Engineers was convened at St. Louis, on the 21st of August, 1867, to consider the question of bridging the river at that place; and to facilitate the examination, the subject was divided, and the several branches of the investigation were referred to committees.

The following named gentlemen composed the Committee on Foundations and Piers:

E. S. Chesbrough,	Geo. A. Parker,
Wm. J. McAlpine,	L. J. Fleming,
Gen. W. S. Smith,	C. L. McAlpine.

The committee met at 5½ P. M. Present—Messrs. Chesbrough, W. J. McAlpine, Gen. Smith, and C. L. McAlpine.

On motion, Mr. Chesbrough was unanimously elected Chairman, and C. L. McAlpine, Secretary, and was requested to make notes of the observations of the members under the direction of the chairman.

It was decided that the discussion should be with open doors, and that any member of the Convention, or any person interested in the subject who expressed a desire to that effect, should be invited to be present during the discussions.

Messrs. T. J. Homer and J. B. Moulton, of Committee on the "Regimen of the River and the character of its Bed," were invited to attend, when they stated to the committee the results of their own investigations, and that of others, extending over a course of many years, as to the following among other points, namely: The periods and action of the floods in the Mississippi river; the character of the material forming the bed and sides of the stream; the disposition and amount of scouring and silting, and the causes, so far as came within their observation; their opinion as to the extent of the same that would be due to the erection of piers for the proposed bridge; the movement and effect of ice and ice gorges; and the information gained by Mr. Homer during his soundings and borings in the river and its bed, from the mouth of the Missouri to Jefferson Barracks, and particularly in regard to the certainty that the rock found below the bed of the river, at the depth shown on his cross sections, was rock in place and not boulders.

The practical experience of the members of the committee in the construction of works similar to the one proposed, the recorded experience of eminent engineers in this and other countries, and the particular information obtained in regard to the case in question, was dwelt upon with great care and deliberation by the committee. Many plans of the latest improvements for foundations and piers were brought forward for discussion. Among the first considered were those of coffer dams. Allusion was made to several that had been constructed in deep water, and under various difficulties and perplexing circumstances. Among the rest a coffer dam built by Col. Abert on the Potomac river at Georgetown, which was about forty feet in depth; another, built by Mr. Jervis for the Croton Aqueduct, at Harlem river, about fifty feet in depth; another, built for the U. S. Naval Dry Docks, at Brooklyn, by Mr. McAlpine, 50 feet in depth; and several others built in this country and abroad were cited, and brief descriptions given, and their relative merits discussed.

It was finally determined that their use here in the rapid currents, deep water, high floods, and the treacherous nature of the river bed, would be attended with great expense and hazard, except for the west pier, near the low water line, on the St. Louis levee.

The plan of the foundations of the Connecticut river bridge, and others similar to it, were then taken up and fully discussed. These piers were built upon a massive grillage of timber, which was suspended by iron screw rods, and lowered to its place as the masonry was being built upon it. When the grillage reached the bottom it rested upon wooden piles, previously driven, and cut off under water just above the scour line of the bed of the river.

In the discussion of the subject of wooden piles, the absence was felt of complete data in text-books or elsewhere as to the amount of safe weight which may be imposed upon piles. All of the recorded experiments are so meagre that engineers have found themselves compelled to make large allowances to keep within safe limits. The committee expressed a desire that the profession would give to this branch of engineering more attention.

Mr. McAlpine furnished to the committee the results of a large number of trials which he had made at the United States Naval Dry Dock, at Brooklyn, which were exactly to the point, but as all of these piles were driven in the same kind of material, the co-efficient of his formula had to be changed to correspond with the different character of the material met with in any particular case in hand, which, said he, might be approximately done by the judgment of the engineer; but the value of this formula would be vastly increased by the acquisition of actual experiments of the same kind on piles driven in the different varieties of earth. His experiments embraced selected piles from nearly 10,000, all of which were driven in a species of quicksand, or at least a very fine micacious flowing sand. A record was kept of the distance which each one of the piles was driven by every blow of the hammer, and also the height from which the hammer fell. The hammers used were of the following weights: 1,200, 2,240, 3,000, 3,500 and 4,500 pounds; and the leaders were from 20 to 57 feet high. In a few cases the hammers were raised by manual power and by horse power, but generally by steam. One of Nasmyth's steam pile hammers of five tons weight, which gave 80 blows per minute, with 3 feet stroke, was also used.

The record of the movement of the piles under each blow furnished the means of selecting such piles for experiment as were best adapted to elicit the information, and to show not only the weight which they would sustain, but also the effect of increasing the weight of the hammers, and the distance of the fall. The trial in each case was conducted by loading the pile with a gradual increase of weight, taking care towards the end of the experiment not to exceed a quarter of a ton at a time, and leaving it on the pile for at least half an hour. It was found in all cases that the more rapidly the blows succeeded each other the greater was the effect upon the pile. Thus the Nasmyth hammer, which struck 80 blows per minute, drove a pile home in seven minutes, which required one and a half hours by the ordinary steam pile-drivers, which struck a blow on an average of once in three minutes, the piles in both cases being similar, and driven in the same kind of material.

Mr. McAlpine was here asked for his opinion for this remarkable difference in the result of the action of the two machines, and replied that he supposed it was to be attributed to the vibrations given to the pile by the blow of the hammer, which greatly lessened the adhesion for the time of the material through which it was passing, and that the blows given by the Nasmyth hammer which succeeded each other so rapidly produced this effect.

Mr. McAlpine was also requested to give the result of his experiments in regard to the bearing power of the iron pneumatic pile. He stated that he made the same kind of trials on these piles when driven to a depth of five feet into the earth, and again at ten feet depth, and again at twelve feet; but on trying to get a measurement at fifteen feet depth, failed from the yielding of the support of the fulcrum of his lever, and the great uplifting power of its short arm of more than 300 tons. This experiment gave a co-efficient for gravel, but he gave the opinion that it would be less for iron than it would be for the ordinary wooden piles.

It was ascertained by calculation that two hundred and ten (210) piles, penetrating to a depth of 28 feet below scour line, would be required to give the requisite support to one pier of the proposed bridge and its load.

It was also agreed upon, that in the opinion of this committee provision should be made in all of the plans that might be considered, for a possible scour in the bed of the stream along the side of the piers to the extent of at least forty feet below low water, but to provide for all possible contingencies they would consider this depth to be forty-five (45) feet.

The weight of one of the heaviest piers was ascertained to be about	6,000 tons
And the weight of superstructure, and the moving load which it would have to support	2,500 "
Making a total load on the foundation of	8,500 tons

Or the load which each of the 210 piles would have to support would be $40\frac{1}{2}$ tons.

At this time, (10 P. M.) Mr. George A. Parker, one of the committee arrived and joined in the deliberations. The minutes were read for his information, and also such portions of the opening address of the presiding officer of the Board as related to the consideration of the subjects properly belonging to this committee.

A resumé of the discussion, as far as it had progressed, was made.

Mr. Parker gave his views, which agreed generally with those expressed by the other members on the subjects that had been under consideration. Mr. Parker was then asked for some of the results of his experience in constructing the bridge across the Susquehanna, at Havre de Grace, where some of the piers were built in water 57 feet in depth. A general idea was given of the management and position of this difficult undertaking.

The next subject considered was the action of floods and ice in the Mississippi, and their probable influence on the piers, and the general habit of the river above, at and below St. Louis. This continued until a late hour when the committee adjourned, to meet at 8 A. M., 22d inst.

August 22.

Committee met at 8 A. M.

Present—Messrs. Chesbrough, Wm. J. McAlpine, Parker, Smith, and C. L. McAlpine.

The general subject of Foundations was discussed for a short time by the members, when it was stated that the Board having resolved to meet at 9 A. M., to receive such gentlemen and citizens of St. Louis as felt interested in the proposed bridge, or who had plans or suggestions to offer in regard to it, it was resolved without adjourning that the members of this committee should meet and accompany them to the river. On this excursion the members of the Board examined the several locations which had been suggested for the bridge, and discussed their respective merits.

After the return of the party from the excursion, the committee met, and on motion, Mr. McAlpine, as President of the Convention, by the power delegated to him, was requested to add the name of A. Anderson to this committee, which was done, and Mr. Anderson took his seat as one of the committee.

General Smith was then requested to give the committee a description of the iron pneumatic pile process for forming foundations. The General said it would be necessary to first consider the nature of the material in which such a foundation was to be placed. From the information before the committee it appeared that at a depth of thirty feet below low water a stratum of hard compact material was found. Whatever character of foundation reaches to and below this, and so gets beyond the reach of the dangerous scouring effect of the river, would seem generally to meet the requirements of the case. This scour has a limit. The velocity of the water usually diminishes rapidly in all deep streams from the surface to the bottom.

Mr. Homer has stated that in all his examinations he has found no sudden depressions or excavations in the bed of the river greater than forty feet below low water, neither alongside of any pier nor near any obstruction which may have been thrown into the stream. The greatest possible scour, therefore, may be considered safely within the limits agreed upon yesterday by this committee. The scour may possibly be reduced by the use of rip-rap.

Mr. Parker remarked at this point that the experience of Smeaton, at Hexham, should induce this committee to use great caution in the reception of the facts and data relating to the changeable bed of the Mississippi river, and that all the circumstances should be well weighed before they are relied upon. The bridge at Hexham was founded upon a bed of coarse gravel, but owing to peculiar circumstances it scoured out to such a degree that the foundations were undermined and the bridge was carried away—"almost the only mistake," said Mr. Parker, "made by this great father of the profession, and frankly acknowledged by him to be so."

A short discussion took place upon the use of rip-rap and other methods for preventing the scour from extending beyond reasonable limits.

Gen. Smith said it will be admitted that a certain velocity or force of impact will carry off, or move or disarrange rip-rap even when formed of the heaviest and largest blocks of stone, and instanced a case that occurred on Lake Michigan, on one of the Government works which he has in charge, where a lower timber of a crib filled with stone, becoming broken by the impact of the huge waves or surf—which continually struck it under high velocity—the stone inside of the crib was rapidly abstracted through the aperture and carried off into deep water. The crib was again filled, but the same result followed.

Mr. McAlpine also cited the well known case at Oswego, where the shore of Lake Ontario is a smooth shelving rock, sloping gradually away into deep water. The Government engineers have at various times attempted to protect a long pier extending into the lake at right angles to the shore by heavy masses of rip-rap composed of slabs of stone from 10 to 15 feet in length, 2 to 4 feet in width, and 1 foot and upwards in thickness. So strong has been the impact of the water upon these heavy masses, that they have been moved to a considerable distance, and their usefulness destroyed. The smooth, sloping surface of the rocky bed of this portion of the lake, on an ascending and gradual rise from the deep water towards this structure, with less friction, and few if any of the irregularities met with at other places, has the effect of concentrating the waval action with more than usual force upon the pier. The problem of a proper protection for this pier is cited by the U. S. engineers as one of the most difficult within the range of their duties.

Gen. Smith resuming, said that although under certain high velocities of water and peculiar circumstances, which made the instances named extreme cases, the employment of rip-rapping did not meet the requirements, yet this kind of protection against the effects of water in motion was too frequently used, in places where it was serviceable, to admit of neglecting its consideration as one of the aids towards securing the bottom of the river near the piers, and that, if there was a certain velocity that would disturb this protection, there was also a certain less velocity at which the stone would not be much affected.

A discussion took place between the members in regard to the uses of fascines of loose brush, alternating with layers of stone, and Mr. McAlpine gave a description of the circumstances under which they were used on the State works in New York, and said that they had been used with very good results in many cases by the State engineers, in places where they had proved economical and useful—answering the purpose designed quite as well as any more costly methods. Its application to the proposed structure, in order to prevent scouring, was a subject which deserved attention; but that until the more complete data was in hand, which would be obtained after the actual commencement of this work, or possibly before that time, this method, as compared with any other, might be left for future consideration.

In this connection, Mr. W. J McAlpine remarked that at the bridge over the Seine, built by Bassompierre, and recently examined by him in company with the engineer, he was informed that the entire width of the river under the bridge, and extending for some distance above and below it, was covered by concrete, which made a perfect protection of the bed of the river against scouring.

Gen. Smith and the Messrs. McAlpine then gave a description

of the process of sinking the pneumatic piles. The same general methods have been employed by Mr. Fleming on the Santee and Pedee rivers, by Gen. Smith on the Savannah river, and by the Messrs. McAlpine on the Harlem river.

Mr. C. L. McAlpine was then requested to describe the pneumatic piles, and the method which was adopted at Harlem for driving them.

The pile consists of a number of hollow cast iron cylinders six feet in diameter, two inches in thickness, and nine feet in length, provided with flanges on the inside by which they are bolted together, one on the top of the other, until the desired length is obtained. The lower cylinder is chamfered on the inside at the lower edge down to about a quarter inch thickness. From a platform on temporary wooden piles, or large scow boats, a derrick is placed which suspends the column and lands it with the sharp end on the bottom of the river in the place where it is to be driven. Another cylinder called the air lock is placed on top of the column, usually made of boiler iron, sides of the same diameter as the columns, with a top and bottom plate of cast iron in which are man-holes that can be closed at pleasure by plates with hinges opening on the lower sides and lined with rubber at the joints. In the top and in the diaphragm or lower plates are cocks, usually two inches in diameter. Leading from the outside of the air-lock, near the bottom, are two curved tubes four inches in diameter, which also pass through the diaphragm and are closed by cocks. The air lock is bolted to the top of the column. Small air pumps usually worked by a small steam engine are connected with one of the curved pipes in the air locks by means of a flexible four-inch tube. The lower man-hole plate is then closed, and air is forced into the column. With the first stroke of the air pumps the operation of compressing the air commences, and as this pressure increases it forces the water out through the open bottom. This continues until the pressure of air equals that due to the head of water outside the column, and the water has all been forced outside. The workmen then enter the air-lock, and closing the upper man-hole a cock is opened in the lower diaphragm, and the compressed air from below is admitted. When the pressure has become equalized the lower man-hole plate falls, and the workmen can pass down on ladders to the bed of the river to excavate the material, which is raised in canvass bags to the air lock by means of a drum, the shaft of which passes through stuffing-boxes to the outside, where it is worked by hand on signal. When the column has been entirely cleared down to the bottom, care is taken to see that no obstructions, such as boulders, logs, etc., remain under the rim of the column.

The workmen ascend into the air-lock, and, closing the lower, the compressed air in the air-lock is allowed to escape through a cock in the upper plate. When the air in the air-lock has become equalized with the atmosphere the upper valve falls, the men pass out, and the bags of material are removed. Men are then stationed at the guy ropes, and the four-inch cock in the curved pipe is opened, and the compressed air in the column allowed to escape quickly. The upward pressure of the air in the column on a surface six feet in diameter neutralizes the weight to an extent which is governed by the depth of the bottom of the column below the surface of water. By allowing the air to escape quickly in the manner mentioned, this weight is suddenly restored with an effect similar to a blow, while at the same time the rapid inrush of water at the bottom causes a complete scouring of the material at and under the sharp rim of the column, and the resistance to driving the column is simultaneously removed.

The friction of the outside of the column against the material through which it penetrates is greatly diminished by the current of water passing along its surface from the river on its way to the inside. If no rocks, trees or similar obstructions are encountered, the column will continue to settle quite rapidly during the time the air is escaping, and afterwards until the material has stopped scouring under the edges, and has compacted itself under the pressure of the water sufficiently hard to sustain its weight. The amount of settling in one operation will frequently amount to ten or twelve feet, or even more.

When boulders or logs are met with, the column stops, and it is then recharged with air. The workmen descend and remove the obstruction, and the process already described is repeated. In this manner columns of almost any dimension may be sunk to any required depth.

The point was raised by some of the members, whether life could be supported at the great depth at which for some of the piers it was contemplated to sink the pneumatic piles, and a discussion was had with those of the members who had used this process, in regard to it.

Mr. C. L. McAlpine was asked to state what he had observed as to the effect of air pressure upon himself and the workmen. He said that in the construction of Harlem bridge, he had been in the habit of entering the columns daily, and frequently, in conducting some of the more important and delicate operations required, has spent hours under air pressure. The greatest depth at which he had been under water was over fifty feet. The pressure due to this depth was about 22 pounds to the square inch over the atmospheric pressure, or, with the latter added, 37 pounds; but this again was frequently increased by the extra pressure required to drive out the water through the compacted material around the outside of the column, so that the pressure was often increased by as much as an additional atmosphere, or about 52 pounds per square inch in all. After entering the air lock, it was closed against the atmosphere, and the pressure equalized with that in the column, in the manner that has been already described; and this operation, and the other one of equalizing with the atmosphere when passing out of the column, were the only times when difficulty was experienced. Men of certain kinds of constitution sometimes suffered greatly, the blood starting from the nose, ears and mouth, and the pain of changing pressure being almost insupportable upon the eyeballs and drum of the ear. These were usually of a very nervous temperament, and excitement would induce them to keep their nerves under great strain, which added to their difficulties. No trouble was experienced in procuring men, however, who could bear the pressure perfectly well without injury. A little practice and familiarity soon accustomed them to the circumstances. The muscular action of swallowing would always relieve the ear drum temporarily from pain and pressure, but after a little practice this was found to be seldom necessary. With new men, the pressure would be let on gradually; but those more accustomed to it, did not hesitate to equalize as fast as their means of doing so allowed, or in a space of less than a minute.

The pressure once fully on, Mr. McAlpine thought it would be difficult, from any bodily sensations, to determine a difference of pressure amounting to at least one atmosphere. The effect, while under pressure, is to cause a feeling of exhiliration, so sensibly felt by the workmen, that a lazy man becomes industrious, and there is seldom occasion to urge any of them in their work. The ventilation is of course excellent, and the operation of breathing becomes so easy that the inhalations are slower and shorter than in the usual atmosphere.

Upon leaving the column and again entering the ordinary atmosphere, the absence of the stimulus of so much oxygen produces a certain degree of lassitude for a time, unaccompanied, however, with any other difficulty. It could not be observed, either in Mr. McAlpine's case, or that of the workmen, that in an experience extending over a year, any effect prejudicial to the health or constitution was produced. Under all the circumstances, Mr. McAlpine thought there would be no difficulty experienced by the workmen in extending the columns to the depth proposed.

Gen. Smith remarked that these piles were capable of great modification in size, shape and material, and are adaptable to the various requirements of different localities, their merits appearing in the most striking manner in situations where almost any other plans in use become costly, difficult and hazardous. Their firmness under heavy loads or shocks by impact of water, vessels, ice, etc., is remarkable. Mr. Fleming, at the Pedee river, had one pile, which had only then penetrated eight feet into the sandy bottom, and which sustained during a freshet a jam of logs and drift wood extending from the pile for a quarter of a mile up the river.

Mr. McAlpine instanced the blow of a steamer coming down with the tide, striking full against a column in the Harlem river, which was unsupported by any bracing, without doing the slightest damage, or causing any movement.

It may be safely taken, then, that these columns will resist any shocks, particularly when braced against each other, and filled with concrete masonry or other material, almost equal in extent to the actual crushing force of the cast iron.

Gen. Smith recommended that, without using the air pressure, a sand pump in open cylinder be used for excavating the inside of the pile, when containing sand, or other material, which is made semi-fluid in water. The air lock may be placed on the column, and the air pressure used whenever a different material is met with, or when boulders, stumps or logs arrest the downward course of the pile.

When working in sand alone, piles have been sunk at the rate of 20 to 25 feet in six hours. Gen. Smith prefers piles of 8 feet in diameter, as he can settle them more rapidly, and they furnish more convenient working room. If these piles are used for the proposed bridge, they can be sunk to such a depth, if necessary, that the iron would crush before the pile could be forced deeper by weight imposed upon it.

Mr. Parker raised the question whether the piles could be relied on to sustain the pier, if the scouring took place to a depth reaching nearly to their lower extremity.

All of the members agreed at once that they would not, because much of their supporting power depends upon the adhesion to the sides of the column of the material through which it penetrates.

Mr. McAlpine mentioned that he had increased the supporting power of the bottom of the pneumatic piles at Harlem by expanding it to three times the area of the true column; this was done by excavating outwards more than two feet beyond the circumference of the pile, and filling in for an extra depth of three feet with a solid mass of concrete; and that this principle was capable of greater extension by the use of suitable iron roof piling.

Mr. McAlpine also stated in this connection that in a comparison of the plans of iron columns with the use of wooden piles, it should be considered—

That the iron piles derive their chief support at a level far below the scour line.

Assume, for comparison, that both descriptions of piles are driven to fifty feet below low water; while wooden piles of fifty feet length, driven in say twenty feet depth of water, obtain their whole support by the whole of the thirty feet of their penetration into the earth,—

If then the scour *should* happen at any one *pier* or *pile* to be ten feet more, that is, to thirty feet below low water, *they will lose*

Not one-third of their supporting power,

But two-thirds of such support.

Because: if two piles are driven, namely, one of thirty feet into the earth, and the other twenty feet, the experience of every engineer shows that the former will sustain *three times* as much as the latter.

If there is *any scour* beyond twenty feet below low water, the wooden piles rapidly lose their supporting power.

Not so with the iron piles, for two-thirds of their support is derived from the area of their base, and hence an additional scour of ten feet does not materially weaken them.

Consequently, the iron piles under this assumed possible and even strongly probable case, will give *twice* or *thrice* the support of wooden piles.

And: If an *extraordinary* scour, even far beyond the extent named, does occur, it does not endanger the safety of the structure resting on the iron piles, while the same scour will *utterly destroy* the supporting power of the wooden piles, and *insure the destruction of the Bridge.*

In the case of the iron piles, the *same scour* will not injure their *really sustaining power* to a degree which would render them inadequate to carry on the traffic over the Bridge;

But will nearly scour out a place in which rip-rap can be placed so as to *utterly prevent evil effect*, and really make the Bridge *perfectly safe.*

That is: The one method has an inherent element of future destruction;

The other, from the same cause, has an element of future safety.

All of the members of the committee agreed that there was no doubt that abundant supporting power could be readily obtained by this process, and that the firmness of a group of piles, as proposed, properly braced, would be amply sufficient to resist the shocks of ice, vessels, etc.

Mr. McAlpine and Gen. Smith both recommended that if this plan was found most advisable, that, instead of stopping the columns at the level of the scour line, and building piers of masonry upon them, the columns should be carried up 85 feet above low water to the level of the bridge seat, as imposing less weight on the foundations, and being far less costly than the use of masonry.

Gen. Smith also recommended for consideration, that, instead of iron piles, wooden columns, square in section, larger at bottom than at top, shod at bottom with cast iron, and loaded to resist the upward tendency of the compressed air, should be used below water, and that, after these columns had been sunk to the required depth, they should be filled in with concrete or other masonry.

Mr. Parker stated that, when it became necessary to build the bridge across the Susquehanna at Havre de Grace, the expediency of using pneumatic piles was considered, but he was deterred from their use owing to the peculiar features of that particular case. He said that the piers of Brunel's bridge across the Saltash were built in fifty feet depth of water, and the excavation below this to the rock was from thirty to forty feet besides. Brunel thought that grouped pneumatic piles at this place were not as suitable as a large caisson, built and worked on the pneumatic principle, and sub-divided into compartments; this caisson was sunk to the bottom, and the masonry built inside of it, under air pressure. At this depth, 80 to 90 feet below surface of water, great difficulties and risks were encountered, but the plan was finally successful. Three years were occupied in constructing this work, which was considered by the committee as very slow progress. This plan was not found to be suitable at Havre de Grace for several controlling reasons, and he was obliged to consider others. He was almost doubtful, indeed, if his piers could have been built at some of the places within reasonable cost and hazard by any other than the method adopted. This was at places where the water was very deep, and swift currents running with a velocity at times of twelve miles per hour; the river also was very broad, in fact, being the northern extremity of the Chesapeake Bay, and liable to storms in which small boats could not live, and was very dangerous for large ones. It was found impossible to excavate the material in all cases down to the rock. Wooden piles were driven at some of these places and left for a time that the action of the currents might be observed, when it was found that scouring took place about the piles to such a degree that their usefulness was destroyed. This scouring effect, however, aided the plan that was finally adopted, by assisting in the removal of the material which overlaid the bed rock. It of course became impossible to place piers on piles in this condition, and that plan was given up. The expediency of using coffer dams had been considered, but they could not be adopted with safety, owing to the peculiar circumstances of the case already named. The deepest coffer dam used on the Thames was twenty-one feet below low water. The tides on this river are sometimes as great as thirty feet. He was strongly in favor, at one time, of using the pneumatic piles.

Mr. Parker then gave a description of the mode finally adopted by him. He stated that each of the nine piers required a different treatment, the circumstances in no two being alike; but the general plan was first to dredge away as much as possible of the material in the bed of the river at the pier site. A three-eighths inch thick boiler iron curb was then sunk and secured in its place. The curb was about thirty feet wide and fifty to sixty feet long, and of sufficient height to reach above the bed of the river. A tell-tale frame work of light timber attaches to the curb, and reaching from it to above the surface of the water, told always the position, inclination and place of the curb. Sand pumps were then used, and the material pumped out of the curb, which gradually undermined, and settled down to the required depth, or on to the bed rock. When stumps, logs or boulders were met with, they were removed by divers working in a bell. After the rock had been thoroughly cleaned off, it was brought to a uniform level by a solid bed of concrete extending over a greater space than the size of the bottom of the pier, using the diving-bell for this purpose. Sometimes there would be a heavy sea, which interfered greatly with the operations. The water in some places was thirty-eight feet deep, and this was increased to fifty-eight feet by the excavation.

Three guide piles on each side, and one at each end, were fixed firmly in position. A strong platform of solid timber, the size of the bottom of the pier, was then placed in position over the curb, and at the surface of the water. On this is placed a caisson of iron large enough to contain the pier, and with sides and ends high enough to reach to the level of high water after the caisson is landed on the bottom. Then this caisson is made water tight. The bottom was then floored over with masonry and stone, and laid in mortar up the sides of the caisson to the top, thus constituting a stone caisson inside of an iron one. This is secured to the guide piles, and the masonry of the pier proper is laid up, the caisson sinking as the weight of masonry inside increases, until it finally settles upon the bottom which has been prepared for it, as already described. It is found necessary to brace this caisson strongly to resist the collapsing pressure of the water on the outside, which, at a depth of forty-six feet, equals nearly one and a half tons on each square foot. The work is done easily, and secured inside the caisson, and it usually occupied only from three to four days to finish the masonry to above the level of the surface of water. At some of the piers screw rods were used to suspend the pier and gearing attached, governed by one man, who at pleasure could raise or lower without assistance the whole pier. In one case it became necessary to relay some of the top courses, and one man raised the pier as high as ten feet. The rock was reached, and the masonry founded upon it at five of the piers. At the other four, after the dredging had been finished, and the curb was sunk to the required depth, wooden piles were driven, and cut off under water by machinery just above the ground, and the platform, with its incumbent pier, lowered upon them.

The plan described is a suggestion to be considered as to its adaptation to the foundations of the St. Louis bridge; but Mr. Parker might vary and modify his opinion, as circumstances and further data and discussion might suggest. He would advise basing the foundation piles on the rock, when it is not at unreasonable depth below the bed of the river.

A practical resumé of the subjects that had been under discussion was had, and it was determined to ascertain, and embody in a resolution, the conclusions at which the members had severally arrived up to this point.

Resolved, That in the opinion of this committee it is both safe and practicable to construct a bridge at St. Louis, of the character of the one which we have had under discussion, with the piers first placed upon foundations of hollow iron piles, driven on the purely pneumatic principle, either to the rock, or, when it lies at too great depth, by an expansion of their base, or driven by the use of sand or steam syphon pumps, or both. 2. Of piers of masonry carried below the scour of the river by the use of iron caissons, as was practised at the different piers of the Susquehanna bridge, and resting on either wooden piles or small pneumatic piles; or 3. By the use of a combination of inverted and direct wood or iron caissons, the inverted caissons filled with masonry by the pneumatic process, and the direct caisson in the ordinary way; and 4. With piers laid up either of solid or galleried masonry; or 5. With the iron pneumatic piles extended upwards to the bridge seat as columns of support, and strongly braced on the lines of the river and the axis of the bridge.

The committee, at this period of the discussion, refrain from expressing their preference in favor of either of the above plans, until further careful estimates have been made upon each, to show their comparative economy, stability and facility of execution.

On motion, the committee adjourned to meet on Friday morning.

FRIDAY, *August* 23.

Committee met pursuant to adjournment, when, on motion of Mr. McAlpine, Mr. Parker was elected Chairman, Mr. Chesbrough having been called away on other business.

The further consideration of the questions involved in the construction of the proposed bridge requiring consultation between the Committee on the Regimen of the River, and that on Superstructure, and in order that some of the general points affecting the calculations of each of the committees might be agreed upon, a conference was therefore had with the two committees named, and a joint meeting was held to consider these points, consisting of the following named gentlemen:

T. J. Homer, J. B. Moulton, H. C. Moore, E. S. Chesbrough, W. S. Smith, Geo. A. Parker, L. J. Fleming, A. Anderson, C. L. McAlpine, S. S. Post, R. M. Shoemaker, O. Chanute, T. B. Blackstone, W. J. McAlpine.

The Chairman of the Committee on Superstructure having made elaborate drawings, estimates and descriptions of plans, and having placed them all before the Joint Committee, the members thereof proceeded to discuss the general subjects, and to compare the results of other experiences applicable to the case so far as to satisfy themselves that the calculations, etc., referred, were substantially correct and sufficient to enable them to proceed with the further general consideration of the questions involved, which were presented by Mr. McAlpine, as follows:

1st. Of the two alternatives for the spans for the main channels allowed by law, which should be adopted?

2d. What spans (within the limits of the law) are the best for the remainder of the distance?

3d. What dimensions and accommodations of bridge are necessary for the convenience of its traffic?

4th. What will be the approximate cost on the basis which shall be decided, in reply to the foregoing propositions?

And the following preamble and resolutions were agreed upon:

Whereas the Federal Law authorizing the construction of the bridge across the river at St. Louis requires, as per Sec. XII., as follows:

Sec. XII. *And be it further enacted,* That the bridge authorized by the preceding section to be built shall not be a suspension bridge, or a draw bridge with pivot or other form of draw, but shall be constructed with continuous or unbroken spans, and subject to these conditions: *First,* that the lowest part of the bridge, or bottom chord, shall not be less than fifty feet above the city directrix at its greatest span. *Second,* that it shall have at least one span of five hundred feet in the clear, or two spans of three hundred and fifty feet in the clear of abutments. If the two latter spans be used, the one over the main steamboat channel shall be fifty feet above the city directrix, measured to the lowest part of the bridge at the centre of the span. *Third,* no span over the water at low water mark shall be less than two hundred feet in the clear of abutments.

And whereas the said law confines the question of the span over the main channel to one of five hundred feet, or to two of three hundred and fifty feet each (clear width):

And whereas, by careful calculation the amount of the materials and the cost of that portion of the bridge above referred to, arranged on the most judicious and economical spans for the remainder of the distance, will involve an extra cost of about three-fourths of a million of dollars:

And whereas there has been no bridge of the character of that which (in our judgment) is required in this place yet constructed, to furnish us with any reliable and certain data on the serious questions of materials and workmanship in spans of such great length: It is therefore

Resolved, That we as practical engineers cannot conscientiously recommend to the parties in interest to venture upon the construction of spans of as great length as the maximum one prescribed by the law, and that therefore we do recommend for adoption the minimum spans allowed by the law as more economical, less hazardous in construction and maintenance, and affording ample accommodation to the commerce of the river and the port of St. Louis.

It was also

Resolved, That, in view of all of the circumstances of this case, we would recommend spans of less than three hundred and fifty feet in the clear, if the Federal law permitted of such reduction.

REPORT

OF THE

COMMITTEE ON THE FOUNDATIONS AND PIERS

OF THE

PROPOSED BRIDGE AT ST. LOUIS.

The committee to whom was referred the subject of "Foundations and Piers," have had the same under careful consideration. It has received valuable aid in its labors from other members of the Board, and from the Committee on the "Regimen of the River." The local knowledge of the latter, and the former investigation by its members of kindred subjects, at once furnished them with important data in regard to that branch of the investigation.

At a later period, a joint meeting was held with that committee and the Committee on Superstructure, in order to consult and determine upon such points as were common to all, and which would form portions of the basis of their separate conclusions. At this joint meeting all that was deemed necessary as pertaining to the consideration of the subjects which this committee had specially in charge was developed.

The members of the Committee on the Regimen of the River stated the result of their own investigations and that of others, extending over a course of many years, as to the periods and action of the Mississippi river; the character of the material forming the bed and sides of the stream; the disposition and amount of scouring and silting, and the causes, so far as came within their observation; their opinion as to the extent of the same that would be due to the erection of piers for the proposed bridge; the movement and effect of ice and ice gorges; and the information gained by Mr. Homer during his soundings and borings in the river and its bed, from the mouth of the Missouri river to Jefferson Barracks, and particularly in regard to the certainty that the rock found below the bed of the river, at the depth shown on his cross sections, was rock in place and not boulders, and the extensive deep borings made by Mr. Moulton at St. Charles, which developed the deposit at that place nearly similar to that at St. Louis. The committee finds that the bed of the river down to the rock is composed of coarse, silicious sand and aluminous and vegetable matter, with an occasional stratum of compact sand and clay. In times of freshets and their subsidence, when the velocity of the current takes a range from six to eight and one-half miles per hour, bringing with it, principally from the Missouri river, vast quantities of sand and other matter, that the extent of the change in the level of the river bed amounts to about twelve feet. In no place for miles above and below the city has the amount of scouring been found to exceed a depth of more than thirty feet below the level of low water, and this depth is regarded as the extreme. The deposits of sand, silt, &c., are usually made when there is a rapid decline of the Missouri floods, and the greatest scouring takes place during a long continuance of a medium Mississippi flood, whose clearer water at a certain velocity takes up and carries with it the turbid deposits brought down by the Missouri.

That part of the river opposite the city, and for a short distance above and below it, is within a range which is peculiarly subject to changes, owing to the various and varying character of the influences of the two great streams above it. These rivers, with their sources hundreds of miles, one to the northward, and the other to the westward, among the great mountain ranges extending above the snow line, pass through many degrees of latitude and longitude, each with its own climate, and when the season of spring storms has passed away and no longer influences the volume of the water, a succession of rises in the river follow from causes operating far away in the mountains to the north and westward, whose storms and melting snows send down volumes of water miles in breadth, and of great depth and rapid current. The fall in the lower Missouri is about ten or twelve inches per mile, and that of the Mississippi six inches per mile. The former passes through hundreds of miles over a river bed and between shores, composed of light sand and alluvium of too little specific gravity to resist the action of the floods, and is carried down the stream (in suspension) in great quantities, the water making great inroads upon the shores and the material of which it is composed, helping to fill the water with all it can carry, until the changes in velocity, eddies, etc., compel it to precipitate this material in the form of bars, new shore lines, or filling up old channels. At every rise, therefore, the Missouri is observed bringing great volumes of material in suspension into the Mississippi; and a flood occurring simultaneously with that of the clearer Mississippi, or a low stage in the former and a high stage in the latter, floods acting jointly or separately, equal or varying in volume or velocity, produce a variety of contingencies attended with the most perplexing results, and without a thorough understanding of the causes named, it would be impossible to form any reliable opinion as to the probable future effect upon that part of the river which it has become the duty of the committee to examine.

At this distance from the mouth of the Missouri river, the bars and channels, aided by judiciously placed dykes, have fortunately assumed a somewhat regular character, varying, it is true, with every change in the stage of water, but within limits that have been carefully observed and noted through a course of years, amply sufficient in extent to enable a correct opinion to be formed as to its future action and habits.

The erection of piers near the channel, and on the bar opposite the city, will be an additional feature in the causes which combine to produce changes in the river bed, and the committee, aware of the grave importance pertaining to this branch of their duties, have given to it a degree of attention equal to that of any other that has been under discussion.

The failure of important structures at other places from this cause alone has been well and carefully considered, and the reasons of such failures duly weighed and commented upon. It has not lost sight of the fact that one of the ablest and most experienced engineers in Europe lost in this way one of the finest structures of the period; and they have endeavored to give especial attention to the dangers here, and in their recommendations to provide against all possible contingencies which might arise to endanger the safety of the proposed structure at this point.

In view of all the circumstances, therefore, the committee resolved that in all the plans of foundations and piers that would be under discussion, the depth of the scouring away of the river bed alongside of the piers should be regarded as equal in extent to forty-five feet below low water. This depth is regarded, under all the circumstances of the case, as amply providing against all possible future scouring; besides which, means will be taken to reduce this scouring near the piers to its lowest possible limit.

A selection of some or one of the well-tried engineering methods for this purpose, to be determined upon as the work of the construction of the foundation develops, can be made to prevent the action of the currents from materially altering the position of the material which supports the foundations and piers. In all of the plans considered, however, the calculations disregard any other support than that which will be obtained below the line of the utmost possible scour, if the material was left or should hereafter become unprotected from the action of the water.

The requirements of the Federal law in regard to this bridge compel the use of piers and superstructure of great size and weight, and even for the least alternative spans permitted to be used more than the usual amount of supporting power must be provided for in whatever plan of foundations is finally determined upon. The law requires that the superstructure over the main channel shall, at its lowest point, be at least fifty feet above the city directrix, or high water. The shortest span permitted over the main channel are two of three hundred and fifty feet each in the clear at low water. The weight of superstructure and piers, under these circumstances, are therefore very great, particularly if the latter are to be built of stone. One of the heaviest of the latter was ascertained to be six thousand tons, if built solid, and the former, with the greatest loads it would have to support—two thousand five hundred tons—making a total weight bearing on the foundations of eight thousand five hundred tons. If this weight was placed upon wooden piles, it would require two hundred and ten in number, each pile being required to support forty and one-half tons.

The satisfactory data before the committee, corroborating the results furnished by Mr. Homer, induce it to rely on the fact of rock in place being found at the depth named, and not boulders. The depth at which the rock is found is as follows: At the west shore the rock is twenty-three feet below low water, the depth of water being the same; at five hundred feet east of this point the rock is sixty-four feet below low water, and the depth of water is fourteen feet; at five hundred feet further east the rock is ninety feet below low water, and the water is ten feet deep; at five hundred feet still further east, the boring was made to sixty-eight feet depth without finding rock, and the water was sixteen feet deep. The great depth at which the rock is found at all places, except near the west shore, induced the consideration of plans of foundations independent of any support to be gained from it, except where it could be reached within a reasonable depth.

The consideration which has been given to the character of the deposit forming the bed of the river, and the changes which it undergoes, and the result of the attempted use of wooden piles in the river, not only at this place, but far above and below it, renders it questionable whether they can be driven so as to give a reliable support to the structure. The resistance of the earth and the strength of the wood will probably limit the depth to which wooden piles may be driven to about thirty feet; and if a scour of ten feet should take place below the top of piles driven through that quantity of material, their supporting power will be so much reduced as to render them nearly useless. It would not be safe to drive them except by previously dredging to the probable depth of the scour, and then the timbers will necessarily be of such great length as to greatly diminish the effect of the blows of the hammer, and give them too little supporting power to sustain the imposed weight. New methods of driving wooden piles have been suggested; but the objections to their use are so great that the committee prefer other plans of foundations which they regard as more reliable for the case in hand.

The necessity of placing the foundations below the scour, and the great rise of the river at each annual flood, would require coffer dams of more than sixty feet in depth, and as these would be very costly and hazardous, the committee cannot recommend their use.

After a careful consideration of the subject, the committee agreed that the following plans would be entirely practicable, with no more risk or uncertainty in their use than is common in such undertakings:

First.—With the piers placed upon foundations of hollow iron piles, driven on the purely pneumatic principle, either to the rock, or, where it lies at too great depth, by an expansion of their base, or driven by the use of sand or steam syphon pumps.

Secondly.—With piers of masonry carried below the scour of the river by the use of iron caissons, as in those built for the Susquehanna bridge, and resting on either wooden or small pneumatic piles.

Thirdly.—With piers of masonry carried below the scour by the use of a combination of inverted and direct iron or wood caissons, the inverted caisson to be filled with masonry by the pneumatic process, and the direct caisson in the ordinary way.

Fourthly.—With the piers laid up either of solid or galleried masonry.

Fifthly.—That instead of masonry the iron pneumatic piles may be extended upwards to the bridge seat as columns of support, and strongly braced on the lines of the river and axis of the bridge.

Although expressing their entire confidence in the safety of either of the plans mentioned, the committee cannot satisfactorily decide without more extended examinations than they are at present able to make, as to which of them it may be best to adopt, and they think it quite safe and proper to leave the selection with the engineer who may have charge of the bridge, as he will have more time and opportunity to procure the necessary data for making comparative estimates of their cost.

In the published minutes of the committee which are here appended, is a description of the mode used in constructing the foundations for the Connecticut river bridge, the Susquehanna bridge, and those at the Pedee, Santee, and Harlem rivers. These include three of the plans named. The results of using one of these plans—that of the pneumatic pile—in European bridges, are also known favorably to the committee.

The inverted caisson placed as deep as dredging can be conveniently carried, and then sunk still deeper, either by pneumatic process, or by the use of sand or steam syphon pumps, would enable the masonry to be carried down to any depth that might be considered expedient, and perhaps do away with the necessity of using piles of any description.

By expanding the base of the masonry sufficiently to obtain the necessary bearing surface, and using concrete or rubble as a foundation for it to rest upon, it may be considered that the object in view, that is, a proper support for the pier and its load, is obtained.

At the joint meeting of the committee, and those on the Regimen of the River and Superstructure, it was unanimously agreed to adopt the plan of the minimum spans allowed by the law for crossing the main channel, namely, two of three hundred and fifty feet each in the clear; and the following preamble and resolutions were agreed upon:

Whereas, the Federal law authorizing the construction of the bridge across the river at St. Louis, requires, as per section XII., as follows:

Sec. XII. *And be it further enacted*, That the bridge, authorized by the preceding section to be built, shall not be a suspension bridge, or a draw bridge with pivot or other form of draw, but shall be constructed with continuous or unbroken spans, and subject to these conditions: *First*, that the lowest part of the bridge, or bottom chord, shall not be less than fifty feet above the city directrix at its greatest span. *Second*, that it shall have at least one span of five hundred feet in the clear, or two spans of three hundred and fifty feet in the clear of abutments. If the two latter spans be used, the one over the main steamboat channel shall be fifty feet above the city directrix, measured to the lowest part of the bridge at the centre of the span. *Third*, no span over the water at low water mark shall be less than two hundred feet in the clear of abutments.

And whereas the said law confines the question of the span over the main channel to one of five hundred feet, or to two spans of three hundred and fifty feet each (clear width):

And whereas, by careful calculation the amount of the materials and the cost of that portion of the bridge above referred to, arranged on the most judicious and economical spans for the remainder of the distance, will involve an extra cost of about three-fourths of a million of dollars:

And whereas there has been no bridge of the character of that which (in our judgment) is required at this place yet constructed, to furnish us with any reliable and certain data on the serious questions of materials and workmanship in spans of such great length: It is therefore

Resolved, That we as practical engineers cannot conscientiously recommend to the parties in interest to venture upon the construction of spans of as great length as the maximum one prescribed by the law, and that therefore we do recommend for adoption the minimum spans allowed by the law as more economical, less hazardous in construction and maintenance, and affording ample accommodation to the commerce of the river and the port of St. Louis.

It was also

Resolved, That, in view of all the circumstances of this case, we would recommend spans of less than three hundred and fifty feet in the clear, if the Federal laws permitted of such reduction.

In addition, it was *Resolved*, That the proper position of the west pier of the two long spans is at or near the line of low water on the St. Louis levee, and that the remaining space between the two long spans and the east shore can be most judiciously filled by spans of two hundred and sixty-four feet each, with spans at each end that will take in the entire width of each levee, unless it shall be found by estimate that the additional expense of the piers is considerably greater than the extra cost of spans of about three hundred and four feet.

It is thought that while for all of the other piers the method of coffer damming would be too costly, yet for the first pier at the low water line on the St. Louis side where the rock is soon reached, it may be adopted advantageously, and the masonry of the pier founded directly on the rock.

The committee examined the estimates of the chief engineer as to the cost of the foundations and piers, and are satisfied that they will be sufficient in amount. The plan on which he has estimated will probably cover the cost of that of any of the other plans, and is taken by the committee as the basis of cost of that portion of the bridge which has been assigned to them to consider. He contemplates a pier located as already mentioned on the St. Louis levee, located on the rock. The next pier will be three hundred and sixty-eight feet east, and will divide the main boat channel. The depth of the rock below low water is forty-five feet, overlaid by about thirty feet of sand, although this depth of material changes with every flood. It is contemplated here to sink iron pneumatic piles of eight feet diameter until they reach the rock, into which they will be firmly secured; upon these, at the level of low water, will rest the masonry. The next pier will be three hundred and sixty-eight feet from the last described, at a point where the rock is eighty-three feet below low water. This will also rest upon pneumatic piles, which, however, will not be driven to the rock, as the cohesion of the material to their sides, and the bearing of their extended bases, will give ample support at a depth considerably less than that of the rock below. The next three spans will be of two hundred and sixty-four feet each, resting also on pneumatic piles. The rock at these points is still deeper than at the other places mentioned, and the supporting power will therefore be obtained in the same way. The next pier being near the east shore, he thinks it may be found advisable and safe from its position to place on wooden piles, cut off below the scour line, but in this estimate the foundations for this pier were regarded as being similar to the others.

A careful revision of the details of the chief engineer's estimate satisfy the committee that a sufficient sum in gross has been arrived at to amply cover the cost of the foundations and piers upon either of the plans which has been recommended by it for adoption at this place. The aggregate amount for these items is $2,541,007.

In conclusion, the committee would say that in their deliberations they have been influenced by a strong professional interest in a work whose magnitude demanded of them the best knowledge, consideration and judgment that could be applied to it. So many peculiar features show themselves here immediately below the confluence of the two greatest rivers that have ever heretofore been presented to the profession to deal with, that they have approached the problem of founding a structure of the size proposed with great caution.

Many of the committee were notified at an early day that this question would be brought before them, and at the meeting it was found that much individual examination of the subject had already been made, assisted by the practical experience which they had gained in the construction of their works. In committee, therefore, a varied and comprehensive knowledge was developed, which greatly assisted in the solution of the difficulties to be met with at this place, and it enabled the members, after free discussion, to arrive at results with great confidence. They now offer them to the Board for its intelligent examination, and would be glad to receive from it any suggestions which may occur to it on the subject entrusted to its charge.

E. S. CHESBROUGH,
W. S. SMITH,
GEO. A. PARKER,
L. J. FLEMING,
C. L. McALPINE,
W. J. McALPINE,
A. ANDERSON.

REPORT OF THE COMMITTEE

ON

SUPERSTRUCTURE AND APPROACHES.

Your Committee, to whom was referred the subject of Superstructure and Approaches of the Bridge, respectfully beg leave to report, that on examination of the charters of the Bridge Company, and the laws of Congress regulating the spans of bridges on the Mississippi river, it is found that the one authorized at St. Louis "must not be a suspension bridge, or a draw bridge with pivot or other form of draw, but must be constructed with continuous or unbroken spans, and subject to these conditions: *First*—That the lowest part of the bridge, or bottom chord, shall not be less than fifty feet above the city directrix at its greatest span. *Second*—That it shall have at least one span of 500 feet in the clear, or two spans of 350 feet in the clear of abutments. If the two latter spans be used, the one over the main steamboat channel shall be fifty feet above the city directrix, measured to the lowest part of the bridge, at the centre of the span. *Third*—No span over the water at low water mark shall be less than two hundred feet in the clear of abutments."

The foregoing conditions are such as do not admit much latitude in the choice of lengths for the spans, particularly when considered in connection with the cost of the necessary substructure, and the fact that the width of the river to be spanned at low water is but about 1,792 feet. Among the alternatives allowed by the law as above recited, the *first* is, that one span may be 500 feet in the clear, while all the others must be at least 200 feet in the clear. If 500 feet should be adopted as the principal span over the main navigable channel, it should obviously be located near the St. Louis shore; and the site of the pier for the support of the western end of this span, should be at or near low water mark on the

St. Louis levee, where a solid rock foundation will readily be obtained. To insure a clear opening of 500 feet between the piers, the length of truss required cannot be much less than 520 feet, making the point of location for the next pier at that distance from the levee, leaving the space to be filled between it and the Illinois shore, 1,272 feet. This space of 1,272 feet admits of being filled with six spans of 212 feet, or five spans of $254\frac{4}{10}$ feet, or with four spans of 318 feet, or with three spans of 424 feet.

The *second* alternative is to build two spans of 350 feet each in the clear, requiring a length of truss of about 368 feet. Beginning at the point of location of the first mentioned pier at low water mark on the St. Louis levee, after putting in the two spans of 368 feet each, there will remain a space of 1,056 feet, which may be filled with five spans of $211\frac{2}{10}$ feet, or with four spans of 264 feet, or with three spans of 352 feet. From low water mark on the Illinois shore to the proper point for an abutment on the east side of the East St. Louis levee, is 160 feet, making the whole distance from the second 368 feet span, 1,216 feet, may be equally divided into four spans of 304 feet each.

The further consideration of this question involves a knowledge of the regimen of the river at this place, and of the foundations for the piers. Therefore, the committee on this subject requested a joint meeting of those to whom these questions had been referred. Such a meeting was held, and after an elaborate discussion of the whole subject, it was unanimously resolved by the members of the Joint Committee, "That, under the circumstances of the case, it is expedient to construct the spans over the main channel of 350 feet in the clear;" and they expressed by resolution, "their unqualified disapprobation of spans of 500 feet." The Joint Committee also recommended the arrangement above described of spans of 264 feet between the main channel and the east shore.

It was proved in joint committee that the cost of a span of 520 feet will be more than twice as great per foot of bridge as a span of 368 feet, and not less than three times as great as a span of 304 feet; consequently, the cost of one span of 520 feet will be equal to the two spans of 368 feet, and one and a half spans of 264 feet; that is, for the cost of one span of 520 feet, no less than 1,150 feet of bridge in spans of 368 feet and 264 feet may be built.

Two general plans for the superstructure and approaches of the bridge have been considered by your committee, one involving the use of four trusses, and the other of but three trusses for each span. The plan contemplating the use of four trusses, provides a clear space of 14 feet in width between the two middle trusses, to be occupied as a railway, with 4 rails, to accommodate the three different gauges of the lines centering at St. Louis. Between the middle and outside trusses, clear spaces of 17 feet each provide for two carriage-ways, either one of these carriage-ways being of ample width for the passage both ways of street cars, and all the common vehicles of travel and transportation. Outside of all the trusses, two sidewalks, 8 feet each in the clear, with substantial railings, are to be added, making the whole width of superstructure 75 feet.

The second general plan contemplates but three trusses per span, omitting one double track carriage-way, and one sidewalk. In other respects this plan is much like the one first mentioned. Of these two plans, the first seems best adapted to the wants of St. Louis and the public generally, and is therefore the one which the committee would recommend.

Beginning at the low water mark at the St. Louis levee, two spans of 368 feet, and four spans of 264 feet, will span the river to the low water mark on the Illinois shore at Bloody Island; one span of 160 feet will reach from low water mark across the levee at East St. Louis, to an abutment where the embankment to form the eastern approach should also abut. From the point first mentioned, to-wit: the low water mark at St. Louis, one span of 264 feet will reach across the levee to the block on the west side of the levee, and where pedestrians will be furnished with especial accommodations for ascending to and descending from the sidewalks of the bridge, besides the usual means at either end of the bridge of gaining access to them.

Going westerly from the river, a span of 160 feet, and a span of 85 feet will succeed. At this point, the identity of width of the structure, and its general characteristics will end. The railway tracks and the carriage-ways, with the sidewalks, will be carried forward on independent structures: the railway over a succession of 85 feet spans, and of colonnades, on a slightly ascending grade, over the various streets and blocks, for a distance of 1,964 feet, to Broadway. The independent carriage-ways and the sidewalks will have a gradual descent for a distance of 595 feet to the streets.

A map of a portion of the city of St. Louis, showing more fully the location, extent and termini of this bridge as herein proposed, and some details of the plan on a large scale, are submitted herewith.

The maximum moving load assumed for the railway, is one locomotive engine, weighing 88,000 pounds, its tender, 50,000 pounds, and a train of loaded cars, weighing 2,184 pounds per foot of the track occupied by the cars; the train being of a greater length than any one span of the bridge. This is believed to be as heavy a load as has ever been made up for a single engine, and heavier than any railroad bridge has hitherto been required to sustain.

The moving load upon the carriage-ways is assumed to be 100 pounds per square foot of an available width of 14 feet, or at the rate of 2,800 pounds per lineal foot of the bridge. On the sidewalks the maximum weight of people that can possibly come, is assumed at 70 pounds per square foot, or 1,120 pounds per foot of bridge. A proper railway track for this bridge will weigh 300 pounds per foot. The timber and plank necessary for one carriage-way, will weigh 560 to 600 pounds per foot. The tram-ways for carriages, and the rails for street cars, bolts, spikes, etc., will weigh about 160 pounds per foot. An allowance for dirt, ice, snow, etc., is made, equal to the weight of snow one foot deep, equal 8 pounds per square foot, or 150 pounds per foot of each carriage-way, including the guard timbers and chords. The weight of carriage-way is therefore from 720 to 900 pounds per lineal foot, according as it may be clear or foul, and the weather may be wet or dry. The weight of a carriage-way floor cannot safely be estimated at less than 900 pounds per lineal foot as a maximum. The weight of the wooden stringers and planks for each sidewalk is estimated at 130 pounds per foot, to which should be added, 80 pounds for snow, ice, mud, and wet weather, making the weight per foot 210 pounds. A suitable iron railing, with proper cast iron bases and angle irons (to connect it to the floor beams), is assumed to weigh 70 pounds per lineal foot.

The trusses of the 368 foot spans at the end posts will be about 2½ feet thick, and the distance from centre to centre of the middle trusses will therefore be 16½ feet. From centre of middle trusses to the centre of the nearest side truss, the distance will be 19½ feet; and the distance from the center of an outside truss to the end of the floor beam, where the railing is to be attached, is 9¾ feet. From the data here given, the weight upon each truss is obtained, and this weight is reduced to pounds per panel, per truss, for convenience of calculating the strains to which the several parts of the structure will be subjected.

Assuming as before that the railing will weigh 70 pounds per lineal foot, or 910 pounds per panel of 13 feet, and that it is attached to the floor beams six inches from their ends, it will operate upon the projecting floor beams as upon a lever, the arms of which are as $9\frac{1}{4}$ and $19\frac{1}{2}$ feet, the weight being applied at the shorter arm. Hence the weight of the railing will give the floor beam at the point of connection with the middle truss, an upward tendency of $\frac{910 \times 9\frac{1}{4}}{19\frac{1}{2}}=432$ pounds nearly, while the downward force at the outside truss will be $910+432=1{,}342$ pounds. Each floor beam is supposed to consist of a pair of solid rolled iron "Phœnix beams," 12 inches deep, and weighing 125 pounds per yard. Each floor beam for the railway being $16\frac{1}{2}$ feet long, will contain 11 yards of this iron, and weigh 1,375 pounds per panel. The floor beams under the carriage-way and sidewalk will be $29\frac{1}{2}$ feet long, containing $58\frac{1}{2}$ feet of the "Phœnix beam," and will weigh $2{,}437\frac{1}{2}$ pounds per panel; the weight of the floor beam which supports the railway track will be sustained by the two middle trusses—one-half by each; the weight of the floor beams under the carriage-way floor and the sidewalks will be sustained by an outside and a middle truss, but the preponderance will be upon the outside truss; the length of these beams will be divided into segments of $19\frac{1}{2}$ and $9\frac{3}{4}$ feet, and their weights will be respectively 1,625 pounds, and $812\frac{1}{2}$ pounds. If the weight of the portion of the floor beams under the sidewalk ($812\frac{1}{2}$ lbs.) be supposed to act at its centre of gravity, it will have a leverage of $4\frac{7}{8}$ feet, against $19\frac{1}{2}$ feet, and will produce an upward tendency of the middle truss of $\frac{812\frac{1}{2} \times 4\frac{7}{8}}{19\frac{1}{2}}=203\frac{1}{8}$ lbs., and a downward force at the outside truss of $812\frac{1}{2}+203\frac{1}{2}=$ $1{,}015\frac{5}{8}$ lbs. The sidewalk railing (if attached to the beam six inches from its end) will operate as upon a lever, the arms of which are $19\frac{1}{2}$ feet and $9\frac{1}{4}$ feet, the weight being applied to the shorter arm. Hence at the middle truss the weight of the railing will give the floor beam a tendency to rise equal to $\frac{910 \times 9\frac{1}{4}}{19\frac{1}{2}}=432$ lbs., nearly, while the force downward at the outside truss will be $910+432=1{,}342$ lbs. The weight of the sidewalk floor, 210 lbs. per foot, or 2,730 lbs. per panel, may be considered as concentrated $4\frac{1}{2}$ feet from the end of the beam, and having a leverage of $4\frac{3}{4}$ feet against $19\frac{1}{2}$ feet, causing an upward force at the middle truss equal $\frac{2730 \times 4\frac{3}{4}}{19.5}=665$ lbs., and a downward force at the outside truss of $2{,}730+665=3{,}395$ lbs. The weight of people supposed to be on the sidewalk is 560 lbs. per lineal foot, or 7,280 lbs. per panel, which, if concentrated at the middle of the walk, will have a leverage of 5 feet against $19\frac{1}{2}$ feet, producing an upward force at the middle truss of $\frac{7280 \times 5}{19.5}=1{,}866$ lbs., and a downward force at the outside truss of $7{,}280+1{,}866=9{,}140$ lbs. The sidewalk will be carried entirely by the outside truss, not only, but it will relieve the middle truss of a considerable portion of the weight of the carriage-way, which it would otherwise have to sustain, and the weight, of which the middle truss is relieved, will be added to the weight on the outside truss. When the sidewalk is loaded, the effect at the trusses will be as follows:

Downward force at Outside Truss.

From weight of railing per panel	1,342	lbs.
" " floor beam per panel	1,016	"
" " floor planks and stringers, per panel	2,730	"
" " people passing, per panel	9,140	"
Total	14,288	lbs.

Upward tendency at Middle Truss.

From weight of railway, per panel	432	lbs.
" " floor beam, per panel	203	"
" " floor planks, etc., per panel	665	"
" " people, per panel	1,866	"
Total	3,166	lbs.

The maximum weight caused by the sidewalk, to which the outside truss will be subjected, is 14,327$\frac{5}{8}$ lbs., while the middle truss will be at the same time relieved of 3,166 lbs. When the sidewalk does not happen to be loaded, this relief will be reduced to 3,166 lbs.,—1,866=1,300.

The top lateral bracing will consist of solid rolled deck beams for struts, and round iron, diagonal tie braces; the bottom lateral bracing will be similar diagonals, connected to the floor beams.

The lateral braces for the railway will weigh about 980 lbs. per panel, and for each double track carriage-way, 1,160 lbs. The weight of lateral braces upon each outside truss will therefore be 580 lbs. per panel, and on each middle truss 1,070 lbs.

Between the carriage-ways and the railway, wooden screens will be interposed, so as to prevent horses from being frightened by locomotives. These screens are estimated to weigh 715 lbs. per panel, per truss. The moving load on one double track carriage-way, $14 \times 13 \times 100 = 18{,}200$ lbs. per panel, will be sustained, one-half, 9,100 lbs., by each truss.

The greatest weight to be carried by an outside truss, and by an inside truss, besides the weight of the truss itself, will then be as follows:

On Outside Truss.

From sidewalk and people	14,327 lbs.
" carriage-way, floor plank, etc., $\frac{13\times900}{2}$	5,850 "
" lateral braces of carriage-ways	580 "
" carriages and horses, $\frac{14\times100\times13}{2}$	9,100 "
Total per panel, per truss	29,857 lbs.

On Middle Truss.

Mean weight per panel, per truss, of engine and cars	14,550 lbs.
Weight of track " "	1,950 "
" carriage-way per panel, per truss, $\frac{900\times13}{2}$	5,850 "
" carriages and horses, $\frac{14\times100\times13}{2}$	9,100 "
" lateral braces and floor beams	1,802 "
" screen	715 "
	33,967 lbs.
Deduct upward tendency from sidewalk	1,300 "
Maximum weight on middle truss	32,667 lbs.
" " " outside truss	29,857 "
Difference	2,810 lbs.

The middle trusses will therefore be subjected to a weight about nine per cent. greater than the outside trusses.

At a future time it may become desirable to place a single track railway on one of the double track carriage-ways, and perhaps upon both. In such a case, the outside truss will be subjected to a load more nearly equal to that upon the middle truss, and it is therefore advisable to make the trusses of the same strength, and alike in appearance.

The spans of 368 feet, 264 feet, and 160 feet, admit of a subdivision into panels of 13 feet each, so that the iron floor beams will be of uniform dimensions, as well as the timbers in the floors of the carriage-ways, sidewalk, railway track stringers, and other parts not specially belonging to the truss. The weight applied to each 13 feet of this truss is therefore taken at 32,667 lbs., as one of the principal elements in computing the strains upon the several parts of each truss. The weight is considered as a constant for each span where the panels are 13 feet, but is diminished or increased in proportion as the width of panel is diminished or increased in other spans.

The weight of the materials which enter into the trusses themselves must be determined for each span separately, and is therefore a variable quantity as regards the spans of different length. The law governing the increase of the strain as the length of truss increases, and by consequence the quantity of material required to resist those strains is quite a general one, so long as the proportions of the truss and the arrangements of the several parts are similar; but it does not apply where the arrangement of one truss differs essentially from that of another. In such a case the strains must be computed for each truss separately, before a tolerably fair comparison can be made.

Figured diagrams of strains, for spans ranging from 85 to 520 feet, were laid before the Joint Committee, of which six of the diagrams were similar in arrangement, but varying somewhat in proportion. These diagrams are herewith presented, together with the formula used in the calculation of those strains.

Detailed and close estimates have also been made of the quantities and cost of material required to fully meet all the strains as thus computed, which detailed estimates have been placed at the disposal of the Illinois and St. Louis Bridge Company, amounting in the aggregate to $3,638,920. This sum, however, includes, besides superstructure of the bridge, as before described, a span of 160 feet, single track, across the Cahokia creek, the embankments of earth forming the approach, paving the carriage-ways, flagging the sidewalk of these approaches, and 6,000 feet of railway track. It is, in other words, the cost complete of that part of the work referred to this Committee.

Respectfully submitted,

S. S. Post,
R. M. Shoemaker,
L. J. Fleming,
O. Chanute,
T. B. Blackstone,
W. J. McAlpine,
} *Committee.*

St. Louis, August 27, 1867.

FORMULA,

BY S. S. POST,

TO ACCOMPANY THE

DIAGRAMS OF STRAINS

SUBMITTED AUGUST 22, 1867,

TO THE

Joint Committee having under consideration the Length of Spans to be recommended in Constructing a Bridge at St. Louis.

[REFERRED TO IN THE PRECEDING REPORT.]

Panel weight per truss of the engine $= W_3$

" " " " tender $= W_2$

" " " " cars $= W_1$

" " " " structure $= W_0$

" " constant quantity$=W_1+W_0 = W$

$(W_3-W)=E=$Excess of panel weight of engine over car weight.

$(W_2-W)=T=$Excess of tender weight over car weight.

Other letters refer to points on the Diagram.

FORMULA FOR THE 368 FEET SPAN, WITH 28 PANELS.

(In this span the braces have inclinations of $\frac{1}{7}$, $\frac{3}{7}$, $\frac{5}{7}$ and $\frac{7}{7}$ of the height, and the secants of their angles are respectively $\frac{1}{7}\sqrt{50}$, $\frac{1}{7}\sqrt{58}$, $\frac{1}{7}\sqrt{74}$ and $\sqrt{2}$.)

MAXIMUM HORIZONTAL STRAINS.

ON TOP.

On A B	$\frac{1}{7}W\times 51\frac{3}{4}$	+	$\frac{1}{196}E\times 100\frac{1}{8}$	+	$\frac{1}{196}T\times 299$
" B C	$\frac{1}{7}W\times 75\frac{3}{4}$	+	$\frac{1}{196}E\times 100\frac{1}{8}$	+	$\frac{1}{196}T\times 299$
" C D	$\frac{1}{7}W\times 99\frac{3}{4}$	+	$\frac{1}{196}E\times 100\frac{1}{8}$	+	$\frac{1}{196}T\times 299$
" D E	$\frac{1}{7}W\times 115\frac{3}{4}$	+	$\frac{1}{196}E\times 100\frac{1}{8}$	+	$\frac{1}{196}T\times 299$
" E F	$\frac{1}{7}W\times 131\frac{3}{4}$	+	$\frac{1}{196}E\times 97\frac{7}{8}$	+	$\frac{1}{196}T\times 299$
" F G	$\frac{1}{7}W\times 147\frac{3}{4}$	+	$\frac{1}{196}E\times 88\frac{7}{8}$	+	$\frac{1}{196}T\times 299$
" G H	$\frac{1}{7}W\times 163\frac{3}{4}$	+	$\frac{1}{196}E\times 88\frac{7}{8}$	+	$\frac{1}{196}T\times 284$
" H I	$\frac{1}{7}W\times 171\frac{3}{4}$	+	$\frac{1}{196}E\times 86\frac{5}{8}$	+	$\frac{1}{196}T\times 263$
" I K	$\frac{1}{7}W\times 179\frac{3}{4}$	+	$\frac{1}{196}E\times 77\frac{5}{8}$	+	$\frac{1}{196}T\times 263$
" K L	$\frac{1}{7}W\times 187\frac{3}{4}$	+	$\frac{1}{196}E\times 77\frac{5}{8}$	+	$\frac{1}{196}T\times 248$
" L M	$\frac{1}{7}W\times 195\frac{3}{4}$	+	$\frac{1}{196}E\times 76\frac{1}{8}$	+	$\frac{1}{196}T\times 227$
" M N	$\frac{1}{7}W\times 195\frac{3}{4}$	+	$\frac{1}{196}E\times 67\frac{1}{8}$	+	$\frac{1}{196}T\times 227$
" N O	$\frac{1}{7}W\times 195\frac{3}{4}$	+	$\frac{1}{196}E\times 67\frac{1}{8}$	+	$\frac{1}{196}T\times 212$
" O P	$\frac{1}{7}W\times 195\frac{3}{4}$	+	$\frac{1}{196}E\times 64\frac{1}{8}$	+	$\frac{1}{196}T\times 191$

ON CHORD.

On b c	$\frac{1}{7}W\times 6\frac{3}{4}$	+	$\frac{1}{196}E\times 18$		
" c d	$\frac{1}{7}W\times 21\frac{3}{4}$	+	$\frac{1}{196}E\times 87$		
" d e	$\frac{1}{7}W\times 38\frac{3}{4}$	+	$\frac{1}{196}E\times 87$	+	$\frac{1}{196}T\times 110$
" e f	$\frac{1}{7}W\times 61\frac{3}{4}$	+	$\frac{1}{196}E\times 84\frac{3}{4}$	+	$\frac{1}{196}T\times 257$
" f g	$\frac{1}{7}W\times 84\frac{3}{4}$	+	$\frac{1}{196}E\times 75\frac{3}{4}$	+	$\frac{1}{196}T\times 257$
" g h	$\frac{1}{7}W\times 107\frac{3}{4}$	+	$\frac{1}{196}E\times 75\frac{3}{4}$	+	$\frac{1}{196}T\times 242$
" h i	$\frac{1}{7}W\times 122\frac{3}{4}$	+	$\frac{1}{196}E\times 73\frac{1}{2}$	+	$\frac{1}{196}T\times 221$
" i k	$\frac{1}{7}W\times 137\frac{1}{4}$	+	$\frac{1}{196}E\times 64\frac{1}{2}$	+	$\frac{1}{196}T\times 221$
" k l	$\frac{1}{7}W\times 152\frac{3}{4}$	+	$\frac{1}{196}E\times 64\frac{1}{2}$	+	$\frac{1}{196}T\times 206$
" l m	$\frac{1}{7}W\times 167\frac{3}{4}$	+	$\frac{1}{196}E\times 62\frac{1}{4}$	+	$\frac{1}{196}T\times 185$
" m n	$\frac{1}{7}W\times 174\frac{3}{4}$	+	$\frac{1}{196}E\times 53\frac{1}{4}$	+	$\frac{1}{196}T\times 185$
" n o	$\frac{1}{7}W\times 181\frac{3}{4}$	+	$\frac{1}{196}E\times 53\frac{1}{4}$	+	$\frac{1}{196}T\times 170$
" o p	$\frac{1}{7}W\times 188\frac{3}{4}$	+	$\frac{1}{196}E\times 51$	+	$\frac{1}{196}T\times 149$
" p p	$\frac{1}{7}W\times 195\frac{3}{4}$	+	$\frac{1}{196}E\times 47\frac{1}{4}$	+	$\frac{1}{196}T\times 149$

MAXIMUM STRAINS ON TIE BRACES.

On L p $\sqrt{2}\ (W_3+\frac{21+15+9+3}{112}W\ +\ W_0)$

" K o $\sqrt{2}\ (W_2+\frac{31}{56}(W_3-W_2)\ +\ \frac{23+17+11+5}{56}W_1\ +\ W_0)$

" I n $\sqrt{2}\ (W_1+\frac{33}{56}(W_3-W_1)\ +\ \frac{19+13+7+\frac{3}{4}}{56}W_1\ +\ W_0)$

" H m $\sqrt{2}\ (\ W+\frac{35}{56}E+\frac{15+9+3}{112}.W_1)$

" G l $\sqrt{2}\ (\ 2W+\frac{37}{56}E+\frac{15+9+9}{112}W_1)$

" F k $\sqrt{2}\ (\ 2W+\frac{39}{56}E+\ \frac{11+5}{56}W_1)$

" E i $\sqrt{2}\ (\ 2W+\frac{41}{56}E+\frac{13+7+\frac{3}{4}}{56}W\ )$

" D h $\sqrt{2}\ (\ 2W+\frac{43}{56}E+\ \frac{9+3}{112}\ W\ )$

" C g $\sqrt{2}\ (\ 3W+\frac{45}{56}E+\ \frac{9+3}{112}\ W\ )$

" B f $\sqrt{2}\ (\ 3W+\frac{47}{53}E+\ \frac{5}{56}\ W\ )$

" A e $\sqrt{2}\ (\ 3W+\frac{49}{53}E+\ \frac{3}{224}\ W\ )$

" A d $\frac{1}{7}\sqrt{74}\ (\ 3W+\frac{51}{53}E+\ \frac{3}{112}\ W\ )$

" A c $\frac{1}{7}\sqrt{58}\ (\ 4W+\frac{55}{56}E)$

" A b $\frac{1}{7}\sqrt{50}\ (3\frac{3}{4}W+\frac{55}{56}E)$

MAXIMUM STRAINS ON STRUT BRACES.

On P p $\frac{1}{7}\sqrt{50}\ \ (W_3+\frac{21+15+9+3}{112}W)$

" O o $\frac{1}{7}\sqrt{50}\ \ (W_2+\frac{31}{56}(W_3-W_2)+\frac{23+17+11+}{56}\ W_1)$

" N n $\frac{1}{7}\sqrt{50}\ \ (W_1+\frac{33}{56}(W_3-W_1)+\ \frac{19+13+7+\frac{3}{4}}{56}\ W_1)$

" M m $\frac{1}{7}\sqrt{50}\ \ (W_1+\frac{25}{56}(W_3-W_1)+\ \ \frac{15+9+3}{112}\ \ W_1)$

" L l $\frac{1}{7}\sqrt{50}\ \ (W_3+\frac{21+15+9+3}{112}W_1\ +W_0)$

" K k $\frac{1}{7}\sqrt{50}\ \ (W_2+\frac{31}{56}(W_2-W_1\ +W_0)$

" I i $\frac{1}{7}\sqrt{50}\ \ (W\ +\frac{33}{56}(W_3-W_1)\quad)$

" H h $\frac{1}{7}\sqrt{50}\ \ (W\ +\frac{35}{56}(W_3-W_1)\quad)$

" G g $\frac{1}{7}\sqrt{50}\ (2W+\frac{37}{56}(W_3-W_1)\quad)$

" F f $\frac{1}{7}\sqrt{50}\ (2W+\frac{39}{56}(W_3-W_1)\quad)$

" E e $\frac{1}{7}\sqrt{50}\ (2W+\frac{41}{56}(W_3-W_1)\quad)$

" D d $\frac{1}{7}\sqrt{50}\ (2W+\frac{43}{56}(W_3-W_1)\quad)$

" C c $\frac{1}{7}\sqrt{50}\ (3W+\frac{45}{56}(W_3-W_1)\quad)$

" B b $\frac{1}{7}\sqrt{50}\ (3W+\frac{47}{56}(W_3-W_1)\quad)$

MAXIMUM STRAINS ON COUNTER BRACES.

		DIRECT ACTION.	REACTION.
On	B′ a′	nothing..	$\frac{1}{7}\sqrt{53}\ (3\frac{3}{4}W_1+\frac{55}{56}(W_3-W_1)\quad)$
"	C′ a′	"	$\frac{1}{7}\sqrt{65}\ (4\ W_1+\frac{53}{56}(W_3-W_1)\quad)$
"	D′ a′	"	$\frac{1}{7}\sqrt{85}\ (3\ W_1+\frac{51}{56}(W_3-W_1)\quad)$
"	E′ b′	$\sqrt{2}\ (\frac{3}{4}\times\frac{1}{56}W_3)$..	$\sqrt{2}\ (3\ W_1+\frac{49}{56}(W_3-W_1)\quad)$
"	F′ c′	$\sqrt{2}\ (\frac{3}{56}W_3)$..	$\sqrt{2}\ (3\ W_1+\frac{47}{56}(W_3-W_1)\quad)$
"	G′ d′	$\sqrt{2}\ (\frac{5}{56}W_3)$..	$\sqrt{2}\ (3\ W_1+\frac{45}{56}(W_3-W_1)+\frac{3}{224}W_1)$
"	H′ e′	$\sqrt{2}\ (\frac{7}{56}W_3+\frac{2}{224}W_2)$	$\sqrt{2}\ (2\ W_1+\frac{43}{56}(W_3-W_1)+\frac{3}{56}W_1)$
"	I′ f′	$\sqrt{2}\ (\frac{9}{56}W_3+\frac{3}{56}W_2)$	$\sqrt{2}\ (2\ W_1+\frac{41}{56}(W_3-W_1)+\frac{5}{56}W_1)$
"	K g	$\sqrt{2}\ (\frac{11}{56}W_3+\frac{5}{56}W_2)$	$\sqrt{2}\ (2\ W_1+\frac{39}{56}(W_3-W_1)+\frac{7\frac{3}{4}}{56}W_1)$
"	L′ h′	$\sqrt{2}\ (\frac{13}{56}W_3+\frac{7}{56}W_2+\frac{3}{224}W_1)$..	$\sqrt{2}\ (2\ W_1+\frac{37}{56}(W_3-W_1)+\frac{12}{56}W_1)$
"	M′ i′	$\sqrt{2}\ (\frac{15}{56}W_3+\frac{9}{56}W_2+\frac{3}{56}W_1)$..	$\sqrt{2}\ (\quad W+\frac{35}{56}(W_3-W_1)+\frac{16}{56}W_1)$
"	N′ k′	$\sqrt{2}\ (\frac{17}{56}W_3+\frac{11}{56}W_2+\frac{5}{56}W_1)$..	$\sqrt{2}\ (\quad W_1+\frac{33}{56}(W_3-W_1)+\frac{20\frac{3}{4}}{56}W_1)$
"	O′ l′	$\sqrt{2}\ (\frac{19}{56}W_3+\frac{13}{56}W_2+\frac{7\frac{3}{4}}{56}W_1)$..	$\sqrt{2}\ (\quad W_1+\frac{31}{56}(W_3-W_1)+\frac{27}{112}W_1)$
"	P m′	$\sqrt{2}\ (\frac{21}{56}W_3+\frac{15}{56}W_2+\frac{9+3}{56}W_1)$..	$\sqrt{2}\ (\quad W+\frac{21+15+9+3}{112}W_1)$
"	O n′	$\sqrt{2}\ (\frac{23}{56}W_3+\frac{17}{56}W_2+\frac{11+5}{56}W_1)$..	$\sqrt{2}\ (\frac{23}{56}W_3+\frac{17}{56}W_2+\frac{16}{56}W_1)$
"	N o′	$\sqrt{2}\ (\frac{25}{56}W_3+\frac{19}{56}W_2+\frac{13+7+\frac{3}{4}}{56}W_1)$..	$\sqrt{2}\ (\frac{25}{56}W_3+\frac{19}{56}W_2+\frac{20\frac{3}{4}}{56}W_1)$
"	M p′	$\sqrt{2}\ (\frac{27}{56}W_3+\frac{21}{56}W_2+\frac{15+9+3}{56}W_1)$..	$\sqrt{2}\ (\frac{27}{56}W_3+\frac{21}{56}W_2+\frac{27}{56}W_1)$

368 FEET SPAN.

RESULTS OF FORMULÆ FOR 28 PANELS.

VALUES ASSUMED.

$W_3 = 18{,}424$ lbs.; $W_2 = 16{,}856$ lbs.; $W_1 = 13{,}720$ lbs.
$W_0 = 47{,}915$ lbs.; $W = 47{,}915 + 13{,}720 = 61{,}635$ lbs.
$(W_3 - W_1) = E = 18{,}424 - 13{,}720 = 4{,}704$ lbs.; $\frac{1}{196} E = \frac{4704}{196} = 24.$
$(W_2 - W_1) = T = 16{,}856 - 13{,}720 = 3{,}136$ lbs.; $\frac{1}{196} T = \frac{3136}{196} = 16.$

STRAINS ON TOP.

On	A B	462,845¾	On	H I	1,518,545¾
"	B C	674,165¾	"	I K	1,588,668¾
"	C D	885,485¾	"	K L	1,658,969¾
"	D E	1,026,365¾	"	L M	1,729,037¾
"	E F	1,166,891¾	"	M N	1,728,821¾
"	F G	1,307,855¾	"	N O	1,728,581¾
"	G H	1,448,493¾	"	O P	1,728,173¾

STRAINS ON CHORDS.

On	a b	nothing.	On	i k	1,217,972¾
"	b c	59,865¾	"	k l	1,349,807¾
"	c d	193,696¾	"	l m	1,481,492¾
"	d e	345,041¾	"	m n	1,542,911¾
"	e f	549,854¾	"	n o	1,604,296¾
"	f g	754,153¾	"	o p	1,503,551¾
"	g h	954,428¾	"	p p′	1,521,178¾
"	h i	1,886,513¾			

STRAINS ON TIE BRACES.

On	A b	238,141	On	E i	186,390
"	A c	273,156	"	F k	184,506
"	A d	232,945	"	G l	183,403
"	A e	207,575	"	H m	95,998
"	B f	268,810	"	I n	104,857
"	C g	268,919	"	K o	112,230
"	D h	181,517	"	L p	102,133

STRAINS ON POSTS AND STRUT BRACES.

On	A a	863,153¼	On	I i	74,898
"	B b	192,007	"	K k	80,164
"	C c	192,085	"	L l	72,952
"	D d	129,655	"	M m	20,170
"	E e	133,136	"	N n	26,497
"	F f	131,791	"	O o	31,763
"	G g	131,002	"	P p	24,551
"	H h	68,571			

STRAINS ON COUNTER BRACES.

On	B a	58,313	On	L h	47,879
"	C a	68,336	"	M i	28,236
"	D a	60,337	"	N k	37,095
"	E b	64,289	"	O l	44,468
"	F c	65,524	"	P m	34,371
"	G d	65,633	"	O′ n	23,481
"	H e	45,993	"	N′ o	26,909
"	I f	50,556	"	M′ p	26,179
"	K g	48,982			

520 FEET SPAN—34 PANELS.

FORMULA, BY S. S. POST,

FOR A BRIDGE TRUSS OF 34 PANELS.

Engine weight per panel, per truss = W_3

Tender weight per panel, per truss = W_2

Car weight per panel, per truss = W_1

Structure weight per panel, per truss = W_0

Constant weight per panel, per truss = $W_1 + W_0$ W

Excess of engine weight per panel $(W_3 - W_1) = E$

Excess of tender weight per panel $(W_2 - W_1) = T$

SECANTS OF ANGLES OF BRACES.

$\sqrt{2} = 1.4142136$

$\frac{1}{7}\sqrt{85} = 1.3170778$

$\frac{1}{7}\sqrt{74} = 1.228903$

$\frac{1}{7}\sqrt{68} = 1.0879676$

$\frac{1}{7}\sqrt{58} = 1.087968$

$\frac{1}{7}\sqrt{53} = 1.0400157$

$\frac{1}{7}\sqrt{50} = 1.0101525$

HORIZONTAL STRAINS ON THE TOP.

On A B $\left(9\frac{1}{4} W + \frac{984}{28} \times \frac{1}{68} E + \frac{742}{7} \times \frac{1}{68} T\right)$

" B C $\left(13\frac{23}{28} W + \frac{984}{28} \times \frac{1}{68} E + \frac{742}{7} \times \frac{1}{68} T\right)$

" C D $\left(17\frac{7}{28} W + \frac{984}{28} \times \frac{1}{68} E + \frac{742}{7} \times \frac{1}{68} T\right)$

" D E $\left(20\frac{19}{28} W + \frac{984}{28} \times \frac{1}{68} E + \frac{742}{7} \times \frac{1}{68} T\right)$

" E F $\left(24\frac{3}{28} W + \frac{966}{28} \times \frac{1}{68} E + \frac{742}{7} \times \frac{1}{68} T\right)$

" F G $\left(27\frac{18}{28} W + \frac{894}{28} \times \frac{1}{68} E + \frac{742}{7} \times \frac{1}{68} T\right)$

" G H $\left(29\frac{23}{28} W + \frac{894}{28} \times \frac{1}{68} E + \frac{712}{7} \times \frac{1}{68} T\right)$

" H I $\left(32\frac{3}{28} W + \frac{876}{28} \times \frac{1}{68} E + \frac{670}{7} \times \frac{1}{68} T\right)$

" I K $\left(34\frac{11}{28} W + \frac{804}{28} \times \frac{1}{68} E + \frac{670}{7} \times \frac{1}{68} T\right)$

" K L $\left(36\frac{19}{28} W + \frac{804}{28} \times \frac{1}{68} E + \frac{640}{7} \times \frac{1}{68} T\right)$

" L M $\left(37\frac{23}{28} W + \frac{786}{28} \times \frac{1}{68} E + \frac{598}{7} \times \frac{1}{68} T\right)$

" M N $\left(38\frac{27}{28} W + \frac{714}{28} \times \frac{1}{68} E + \frac{598}{7} \times \frac{1}{68} T\right)$

" N O $\left(40\frac{3}{28} W + \frac{714}{28} \times \frac{1}{68} E + \frac{568}{7} \times \frac{1}{68} T\right)$

" O P $\left(41\frac{1}{4} W + \frac{696}{28} \times \frac{1}{68} E + \frac{526}{7} \times \frac{1}{68} T\right)$

" P Q $\left(41\frac{1}{4} W + \frac{624}{28} \times \frac{1}{68} E + \frac{526}{7} \times \frac{1}{68} T\right)$

" Q R $\left(41\frac{1}{4} W + \frac{624}{28} \times \frac{1}{68} E + \frac{496}{7} \times \frac{1}{68} T\right)$

" R S $\left(41\frac{1}{4} W + \frac{606}{28} \times \frac{1}{68} E + \frac{454}{7} \times \frac{1}{68} T\right)$

HORIZONTAL STRAIN ON CHORD.

On	a b	(nothing.)
"	b c	$(1\frac{1}{4}\ W + \frac{180}{28} \times \frac{1}{68}\ E)$
"	c d	$(3\frac{11}{28}\ W + \frac{867}{28} \times \frac{1}{68}\ E)$
"	d e	$(6\frac{10}{28}\ W + \frac{867}{28} \times \frac{1}{68}\ E + \frac{280}{7} \times \frac{1}{68}\ T)$
"	e f	$(11\frac{3}{28}\ W + \frac{858}{28} \times \frac{1}{68}\ E + \frac{658}{7} \times \frac{1}{68}\ T)$
"	f g	$(15\frac{15}{28}\ W + \frac{786}{28} \times \frac{1}{68}\ E + \frac{658}{7} \times \frac{1}{68}\ T)$
"	g h	$(18\frac{23}{28}\ W + \frac{786}{28} \times \frac{1}{68}\ E + \frac{628}{7} \times \frac{1}{68}\ T)$
"	h i	$(22\frac{3}{28}\ W + \frac{768}{28} \times \frac{1}{68}\ E + \frac{586}{7} \times \frac{1}{68}\ T)$
"	i k	$(25\frac{11}{28}\ W + \frac{696}{28} \times \frac{1}{68}\ E + \frac{586}{7} \times \frac{1}{68}\ T)$
"	k l	$(28\frac{19}{28}\ W + \frac{696}{28} \times \frac{1}{68}\ E + \frac{556}{7} \times \frac{1}{68}\ T)$
"	l m	$(30\frac{23}{28}\ W + \frac{678}{28} \times \frac{1}{68}\ E + \frac{514}{7} \times \frac{1}{68}\ T)$
"	m n	$(32\frac{27}{28}\ W + \frac{606}{28} \times \frac{1}{68}\ E + \frac{514}{7} \times \frac{1}{68}\ T)$
"	n o	$(35\frac{3}{28}\ W + \frac{606}{28} \times \frac{1}{68}\ E + \frac{484}{7} \times \frac{1}{68}\ T)$
"	o p	$(37\frac{1}{4}\ W + \frac{588}{28} \times \frac{1}{68}\ E + \frac{443}{7} \times \frac{1}{68}\ T)$
"	p q	$(38\frac{1}{4}\ W + \frac{516}{28} \times \frac{1}{68}\ E + \frac{442}{7} \times \frac{1}{68}\ T)$
"	q r	$(39\frac{1}{4}\ W + \frac{516}{28} \times \frac{1}{68}\ E + \frac{412}{7} \times \frac{1}{68}\ T)$
"	r s	$(40\frac{1}{4}\ W + \frac{468}{28} \times \frac{1}{68}\ E + \frac{370}{7} \times \frac{1}{68}\ T)$
"	s s	$(41\frac{1}{4}\ W + \frac{462}{28} \times \frac{1}{58}\ E + \frac{370}{7} \times \frac{1}{68}\ T)$

STRAINS ON TIE BRACES.

On O s	$\surd 2\,(W_0 + W_3 + \frac{27}{136} W_2 + \frac{24}{68} W_1)$
" N r	$\surd 2\,(W_0 + W_2 + \frac{37}{68} W_3 - W_2) + \frac{85}{68} W_1)$
" M q	$\surd 2\,(\quad W + \frac{39}{68} (W_3 - W_1) + \frac{64\frac{3}{4}}{68} W_1)$
" L p	$\surd 2\,(\quad W + \frac{41}{68} (W_3 - W_1) + \frac{24}{68} W_1)$
" K o	$\surd 2\,(2W + \frac{43}{68} (W_3 - W_1) + \frac{24}{68} W_1)$
" I n	$\surd 2\,(2W + \frac{45}{68} (W_3 - W_1) + \frac{33}{68} W_1)$
" H m	$\surd 2\,(2W + \frac{47}{68} (W_3 - W_1) + \frac{30\frac{3}{4}}{68} W_1)$
" G l	$\surd 2\,(2W + \frac{49}{68} (W_3 - W_1) + \frac{13\frac{1}{2}}{68} W_1)$
" F k	$\surd 2\,(3W + \frac{51}{68} (W_3 - W_1) + \frac{13\frac{1}{2}}{68} W_1)$
" E i	$\surd 2\,(3W + \frac{53}{68} (W_3 - W_1) + \frac{16}{68} W_1)$
" D h	$\surd 2\,(3W + \frac{55}{68} (W_3 - W_1) + \frac{7\frac{3}{4}}{68} W_1)$
" C g	$\surd 2\,(3W + \frac{57}{68} (W_3 - W_1) + \frac{6}{68} W_1)$
" B f	$\surd 2\,(4W + \frac{59}{68} (W_3 - W_1) + \frac{1\frac{1}{2}}{68} W_1)$
" A e	$\surd 2\,(4W + \frac{61}{68} (W_3 - W_1) + \frac{2\frac{1}{2}}{68} W_1)$
" A d	$\frac{1}{7}\surd 74(4W + \frac{63}{68} (W_3 - W_1) + \frac{\frac{3}{4}}{68} W_1)$
" A c	$\frac{1}{7}\surd 58(4W + \frac{65}{68} (W_3 - W_1) + \qquad)$
" A b	$\frac{1}{7}\surd 50(4\frac{3}{4} W + \frac{67}{68} (W_3 - W_1) + \qquad)$

STRAINS ON THE COUNTER BRACES.

EFFECT OF MOVING LOAD.

On E′ b′ $\surd 2\left(\frac{3}{4} \times \frac{1}{68} W_3\right)$

" F′ c′ $\surd 2\left(\frac{3}{68} W_3\right)$

" G′ d′ $\surd 2\left(\frac{5}{68} W_3\right)$

" H′ c′ $\surd 2\left(\frac{7}{68} W_3 + \frac{3}{4} \times \frac{1}{68} W_2\right)$

" I′ f′ $\surd 2\left(\frac{9}{68} W_3 + \frac{3}{68} W_2\right)$

" K′ g′ $\surd 2\left(\frac{11}{68} W_3 + \frac{5}{68} W_2\right)$

" L′ h′ $\surd 2\left(\frac{13}{68} W_3 + \frac{7}{68} W_2 + \frac{3}{4} \times \frac{1}{68} W_1\right)$

" M′ i′ $\surd 2\left(\frac{15}{68} W_3 + \frac{9}{68} W_2 + \frac{3}{68} W_1\right)$

" N′ k′ $\surd 2\left(\frac{17}{68} W_3 + \frac{11}{68} W_2 + \frac{5}{68} W_1\right)$

" O′ l′ $\surd 2\left(\frac{19}{68} W_3 + \frac{13}{68} W_2 + \frac{7\frac{3}{4}}{68} W_1\right)$

" P′ m′ $\surd 2\left(\frac{21}{68} W_3 + \frac{15}{68} W_2 + \frac{12}{68} W_1\right)$

" Q′ n′ $\surd 2\left(\frac{23}{68} W_3 + \frac{17}{68} W_2 + \frac{16}{68} W_1\right)$

" R′ o′ $\surd 2\left(\frac{25}{68} W_3 + \frac{19}{68} W_2 + \frac{20\frac{3}{4}}{68} W_1\right)$

" S p′ $\surd 2\left(\frac{27}{68} W_3 + \frac{21}{68} W_2 + \frac{27}{68} W_1\right)$

" R q′ $\surd 2\left(\frac{29}{68} W_3 + \frac{23}{68} W_2 + \frac{33}{68} W_1\right)$

" O r′ $\surd 2\left(\frac{31}{68} W_3 + \frac{25}{68} W_2 + \frac{30\frac{3}{4}}{68} W_1\right)$

" P s′ $\surd 2\left(\frac{33}{68} W_3 + \frac{27}{68} W_2 + \frac{24}{68} W_1\right)$

STRAINS ON THE COUNTER BRACES.

EFFECTS OF REACTION.

On S p $\surd\ 2\,(\ W_3 + \frac{27}{136}\ W_2\ \frac{24}{68}\ W_1)$

" R o $\surd\ 2\,(\ W_2 + \frac{37}{68}\ \ W_3 - W_2) + \frac{35}{68}\ W_1)$

" O n $\surd\ 2\,(\ W_1 + \frac{39}{68}\ \ W_3 - W_1) + \frac{64\frac{3}{4}}{68}\ W_1)$

" P m $\surd\ 2\,(\ W_1 + \frac{41}{68}\ \ W_3 - W_1) + \frac{24}{68}\ W_1)$

" O l $\surd\ 2\,(2\ W_1 + \frac{43}{68}\ (W_3 - W_1) + \frac{24}{68}\ W_1)$

" M k $\surd\ 2\,(2\ W_1 + \frac{45}{68}\ (W_3 - W_1) + \frac{33}{68}\ W_1)$

" N i $\surd\ 2\,(2\ W_1 + \frac{47}{68}\ (W_3 - W_1) + \frac{39\frac{3}{4}}{68}\ W_1)$

" L h $\surd\ 2\,(2\ W_1 + \frac{49}{68}\ (W_3 - W_1) + \frac{27}{136}\ W_1)$

" K g $\surd\ 2\,(3\ W_1 + \frac{51}{68}\ (W_3 - W_1) + \frac{27}{136}\ W_1)$

" L f $\surd\ 2\,(3\ W_1 + \frac{53}{68}\ (W_3 - W_1) + \frac{16}{68}\ W_1)$

" H e $\surd\ 2\,(3\ W_1 + \frac{55}{68}\ (W_3 - W_1) + \frac{7\frac{3}{4}}{68}\ W_1)$

" G d $\surd\ 2\,(3\ W_1 + \frac{57}{68}\ (W_3 - W_1) + \frac{6}{68}\ W_1)$

" F c $\surd\ 2\,(4\ W_1 + \frac{59}{68}\ (W_3 - W_1) + \frac{3}{136}\ W_1)$

" E b $\surd\ 2\,(4\ W_1 + \frac{61}{68}\ (W_3 - W_1) + \frac{5}{136}\ W_1)$

" D a $\frac{1}{7}\surd\,85\,(4\ W_1 + \frac{63}{68}\ (W_3 - W_1) + \frac{\frac{3}{4}}{68}\ W_1)$

" C a $\frac{1}{7}\surd\,65\,(4\ W_1 + \frac{65}{68}\ (W_3 - W_1) + \qquad)$

" B a $\frac{1}{7}\surd\,53\,(4\tfrac{3}{4}\,W_1 + \frac{67}{68}\ (W_3 - W_1) + \qquad)$

STRAINS ON POSTS OR STRUT BRACES.

On S s $\frac{1}{7}\surd 50\ (W_3 + \frac{27}{136} W_2 + \frac{24}{68} W_1)$

" R r $\frac{1}{7}\surd 50\ (W_2 + \frac{37}{68} (W_3 - W_2) + \frac{85}{68} W_1)$

" Q q $\frac{1}{7}\surd 50\ (W_1 + \frac{39}{68} (W_3 - W_1) + \frac{64\frac{3}{4}}{68} W_1)$

" P p $\frac{1}{7}\surd 50\ (W_1 + \frac{41}{68} (W_3 - W_1) + \frac{24}{68} W_1)$

" O o $\frac{1}{7}\surd 50\ (W_0 + W_3 + \frac{27}{136} W_2 + \frac{24}{68} W_1)$

" N n $\frac{1}{7}\surd 50\ (W_0 + W_2 + \frac{37}{68} (W_3 - W_2) + \frac{85}{68} W_1)$

" M m $\frac{1}{7}\surd 50\ (W + \frac{39}{68} (W_3 - W_1) + \frac{64\frac{3}{4}}{68} W_1)$

" L l $\frac{1}{7}\surd 50\ (W + \frac{41}{68} (W_3 - W_1) + \frac{24}{68} W_1)$

" K k $\frac{1}{7}\surd 50\ (2W + \frac{43}{68} (W_3 - W_1) + \frac{24}{68} W_1)$

" I i $\frac{1}{7}\surd 50\ (2W + \frac{45}{68} (W_3 - W_1) + \frac{33}{68} W_1)$

" H h $\frac{1}{7}\surd 50\ (2W + \frac{47}{68} (W_3 - W_1) + \frac{39\frac{3}{4}}{68} W_1)$

" G g $\frac{1}{7}\surd 50\ (2W + \frac{49}{68} (W_3 - W_1) + \frac{27}{136} W_1)$

" F f $\frac{1}{7}\surd 50\ (3W + \frac{51}{68} (W_3 - W_1) + \frac{27}{136} W_1)$

" E e $\frac{1}{7}\surd 50\ (3W + \frac{53}{68} (W_3 - W_1) + \frac{16}{68} W_1)$

" D d $\frac{1}{7}\surd 50\ (3W + \frac{55}{68} (W_3 - W_1) + \frac{7\frac{3}{4}}{68} W_1)$

" C c $\frac{1}{7}\surd 50\ (3W + \frac{57}{68} (W_3 - W_1) + \frac{3}{136} W_1)$

" B b $\frac{1}{7}\surd 50\ (4W + \frac{59}{68} (W_3 - W_1) + \frac{5}{136} W_1)$

" A a $16\frac{3}{4} W + \frac{115\frac{3}{4}}{68} (W_3 - W_1) + \frac{124}{68} (W_2 - W_1)$

520 FEET SPAN.

RESULTS OF FORMULÆ FOR 34 PANELS.

VALUES ASSUMED.

$W_3 = 19,584$ lbs.; $W_2 = 17,680$ lbs.; $W_1 = 16,388$ lbs.
$W_0 = 87,240$ lbs.; $W = 87,240 + 16,388 = 103,628$ lbs.
$(W_3 - W_1) = E = 19,584 - 16,388 = 3,196$; $\frac{1}{68} E = \frac{3196}{68} = 47$ lbs.
$(W_2 - W_1) = T = 17,680 - 16,388 = 1,292$; $\frac{1}{68} T = \frac{1292}{68} = 19$ lbs.

STRAINS ON TOP.

On A B	962,219$\frac{19}{28}$	On K L	3,804,008$\frac{19}{28}$
" B C	1,435,937$\frac{19}{28}$	" L M	3,923,296$\frac{13}{28}$
" C D	1,791,243$\frac{19}{28}$	" M N	4,040,607$\frac{17}{28}$
" D E	2,146,539$\frac{19}{28}$	" N O	4,158,958$\frac{5}{28}$
" E F	2,501,805$\frac{13}{28}$	" O P	4,277,245$\frac{27}{28}$
" F G	2,856,980$\frac{17}{28}$	" P Q	4,277,125$\frac{3}{28}$
" G H	3,093,763$\frac{5}{28}$	" Q R	4,277,043$\frac{19}{28}$
" H I	3,330,482$\frac{27}{28}$	" R S	4,276,899$\frac{13}{28}$
" I K	3,567,226$\frac{3}{28}$		

STRAINS ON CHORD.

On a b	nothing.	On k l	2,974,580$\frac{12}{28}$
" b c	129,837$\frac{4}{28}$	" l m	3,196,496$\frac{6}{28}$
" c d	353,065$\frac{11}{28}$	" m n	3,418,435$\frac{10}{28}$
" d e	694,317$\frac{11}{28}$	" n o	3,640,413$\frac{26}{28}$
" e f	1,154,277$\frac{6}{28}$	" o p	3,862,333$\frac{5}{28}$
" f g	1,613,040$\frac{10}{28}$	" p q	3,965,836$\frac{24}{28}$
" g h	1,953,450$\frac{26}{28}$	" q r	4,069,383$\frac{12}{28}$
" h i	2,293,798$\frac{20}{28}$	" r s	4,172,867$\frac{6}{28}$
" i k	2,634,257$\frac{26}{28}$	" s s′	4,276,434$\frac{22}{28}$

STRAINS ON TIE BRACES.

On A b	499,616	On G l	300,965
" A c	454,299	" H m	309,804
" A d	513,256	" I n	307,351
" A e	591,972	" K o	304,145
" B f	590,646	" L p	158,558
" C g	445,494	" M q	171,355
" D h	445,957	" N r	178,916
" E i	448,636	" O s	164,317
" F k	447,651		

STRAINS ON POSTS AND STRUT BRACES.

On A a	1,743,541$\frac{3}{4}$	On K k	217,245
" B b	421,887	" L l	112,469
" C c	318,207	" M m	122,331
" D d	318,538	" N n	127,735
" E e	320,452	" O o	117,297
" F f	319,748	" P p	24,343
" G g	214,974	" Q q	34,205
" H h	221,391	" R r	39,599
" I i	219,531	" S s	29,171

STRAINS ON COUNTER BRACES.

On B a	83,414	On M i	63,050
" C a	80,703	" N k	60,597
" D a	90,476	" O l	57,391
" E b	98,464	" P m	34,081
" F c	97,138	" Q n	47,888
" G d	75,363	" R o	55,439
" H e	75,286	" S p	40,840
" I f	78,505	" R′ q	28,720
" K g	77,520	" Q′ r	35,367
" L h	54,211	" P′ s	31,516

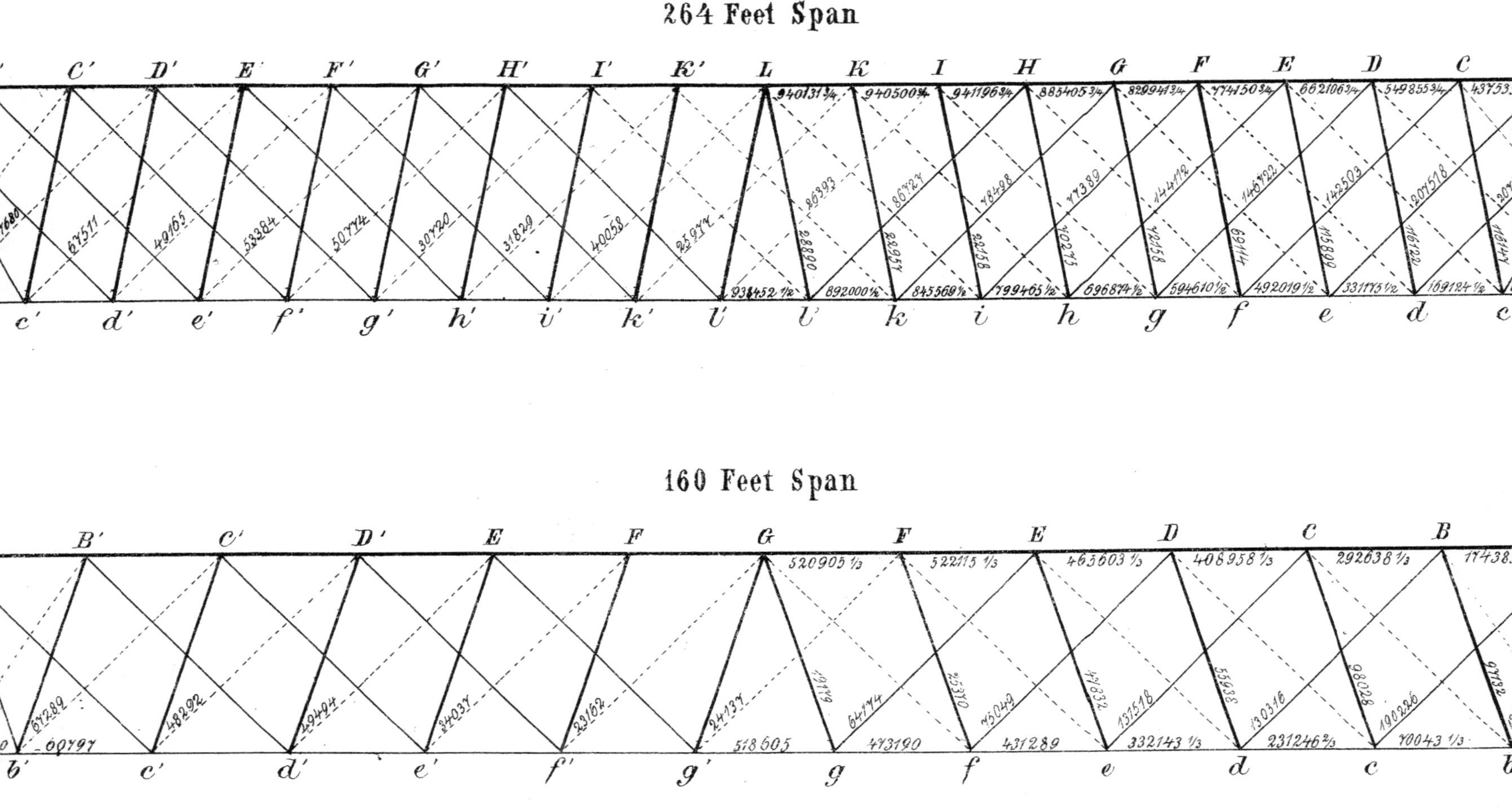
264 Feet Span
C' D' E' F' G' H' I' K' L K I H G F E D C
9401313/4
9405003/4
9411963/4
8854053/4
8299413/4
7741503/4
6621063/4
5498553/4
938452 1/2
892000 1/2
845569 1/2
799465 1/2
696874 1/2
594610 1/2
492019 1/2
331175 1/2
169124 1/2
c' d' e' f' g' h' i' k' l' l' k i h g f e d c
160 Feet Span
B' C' D' E F G F E D C B
520905 1/3
522115 1/3
463603 1/3
408958 1/3
292638 1/3
174385
518605
473190
431289
332143 1/3
231246 2/3
100431/3
b' c' d' e' f' g' g f e d c b

304 Feet Span

85 Feet Span

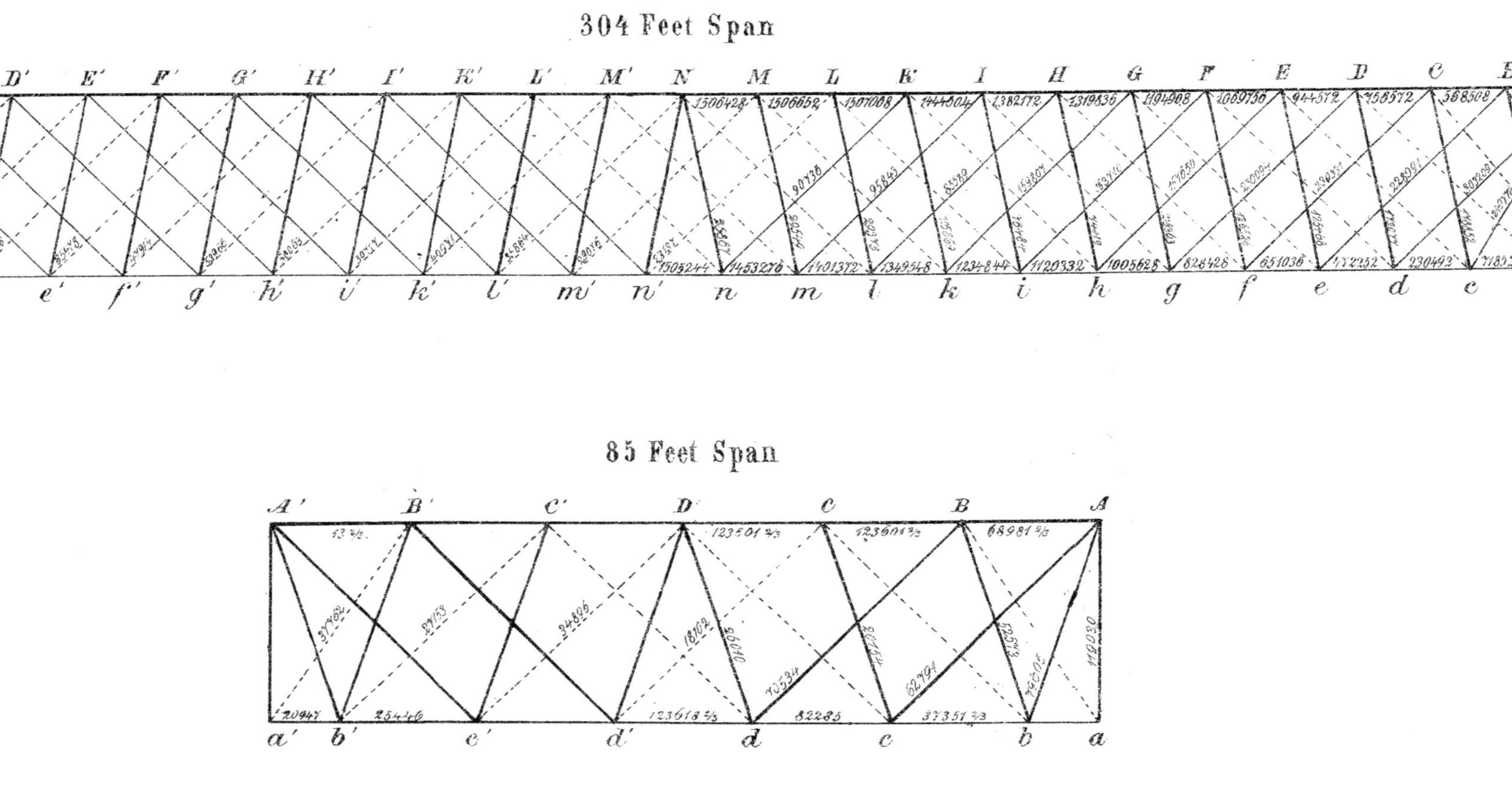

REPORT OF COMMITTEE

ON

COMMERCE CROSSING THE BRIDGE.

To the Convention of Engineers,
assembled at St. Louis, August, 1867.

Your committee to whom was referred the "Commerce crossing the Bridge" have not been able to ascertain with entire accuracy, in tons, the amount of traffic of the railroads centering at St. Louis from the west, as the reports of the railroad companies give their receipts in money, and omit to state their tonnage. All these railroads are being rapidly extended, and their receipts will increase at a much more rapid rate; their tonnage will very soon exceed, if it does not already, that of the Illinois railroads centering at this point.

The number of tons of freight of all kinds received at St. Louis in 1866, by the Illinois railroads, and the number of tons exported from St. Louis by those railroads during the same year, as shown by the reports of those Companies, amount to $470,603\frac{608}{2000}$ tons, exclusive of coal, for which, add $544,525\frac{1520}{2000}$ tons. The arrivals at and departures from St. Louis by the Illinois railroads in 1866, as appears by the reports, was no less than 479,000 persons, or 656 each way daily.

Of the flour and grain received at St. Louis, by wagons, in 1866, amounting to 35,430 tons, the greater portion came from Illinois, and indicates, in some degree, the traffic across the river by means of such vehicles.

The population of St. Clair and adjacent counties in Illinois, numbered in 1860 and 1865:

	1860.	1865.
St. Clair County	37,694	43,701
Madison "	31,215	47,042
Clinton "	10,941	13,795
Washington "	13,737	17,193
Total in four counties	93,587	121,691

showing an increase of over 30 per cent. in five years. St. Clair county and the southern part of Madison county lie upon the river directly opposite St. Louis. They are all among the richest agricultural counties of the State, and will largely contribute to the highway traffic of the bridge. The very large traffic in 1866 between St. Louis and the Illinois shore opposite, already noticed, shows the importance of a bridge across the river at this point; but when the rapid increase in the length of the railroad lines west of the Mississippi, and the consequent increase in the population and business of St. Louis, is considered, the *absolute necessity* of the bridge being constructed *at once* will be seen.

In 1866 there were but 940 miles of railroad in the State of Missouri, of which but 628 miles contributed directly to St. Louis.

A bridge over the Mississippi river at Quincy is now being constructed, as the outlet of the Hannibal and St. Joseph R.R., for 209 miles of the 312 miles in Missouri not centering at St. Louis.

The North Missouri R.R., however, intersects the Hannibal and St. Joseph R.R. at Macon, a point 73 miles westward of Quincy, and by this connection a large part of the business from the west seeking a passage of the Mississippi at Quincy, would be directed to St. Louis if permitted to cross the river there upon a bridge. The North Missouri R.R. at present extends to Atlanta, 12 miles from Macon, and is under contract to the Iowa State line, 53 miles farther.

The Iowa Central R.R. Company has also under contract an extension of this line for 150 miles northward from the Iowa State line, which will ere long connect with all the main trunk lines crossing the country from the west to the Mississippi river, and extending to St. Paul, Minnesota, affording a heavy winter traffic when the river is closed.

The Cedar Rapids R.R., making similar connections with St. Paul, and running south from Ottumwa, terminates by a connection with the North Missouri at Iowa State line. Both of these roads in Iowa are in a forward state of construction. A principal branch of the North Missouri R.R. is also being built from Moberly, a point 145 miles from St. Louis, to Leavenworth and Kansas City.

The Pacific R.R. of Missouri is completed to Kansas City and Leavenworth.

The Union Pacific Railway, E. D., has recently been opened 260 miles from Kansas City and Wyandott, including a branch of 33 miles from Leavenworth to Lawrence, and will be extended 140 miles farther this year, making 400 miles beyond Kansas City to be in operation before the close of 1867. This Railway will have its western terminus at San Francisco. Its construction is in the hands of responsible capitalists who are pushing the work with astonishing rapidity. The traffic of this immense road will naturally pass over the St. Louis bridge.

The Iron Mountain R.R. will be extended to Memphis; and it will not be many years before a railroad from East St. Louis to Cairo direct will be completed.

The Atlantic and Pacific Railway (formerly the Southwest Branch of the Missouri Pacific R.R.,) connects with the Missouri Pacific at Franklin, 37 miles from St. Louis, and is in operation from that point to the Gasconade river, 90 miles, or 127 miles from St. Louis. This road will pass through the best agricultural and mining lands of the State of Missouri, and is destined to be extended to the Pacific coast.

The Central Branch Union Pacific R.R. is being built west to Denver City, and will connect with the Union Pacific Railway.

The Cairo and Fulton R.R. will ultimately be extended through Arkansas and Texas, and a large portion of the trade of those States will center at St. Louis.

A railroad is being constructed south from Kansas City to Galveston, Texas, the traffic of which will be directed to St. Louis.

The St Louis, Jacksonville and Chicago R.R. is developing a large traffic, which is now almost exclusively with St. Louis. This road will be opened to Bloomington, 180 miles from St. Louis, about October 1st, 1867.

It is reported that the Railroad from Terre Haute, via Vandalia, to St. Louis is under contract.

The coal brought in by the Illinois railroads is but a portion of the whole quantity received at East St. Louis and Illinoistown. Nearly all the coal brought to the river has to be dumped from the cars or wagons into the boats, transported across the river, and then taken out and reloaded upon wagons or carts, and hauled in that manner to its destination. The shrinkage, or loss, occasioned by this unloading and reloading is acknowledged by the dealers to amount to no less than 5 per cent.

At Rock Island and Clinton the rates of transportation are from 70 cents to $1 per ton.

When the bridge shall have been completed, the highway travel and traffic will increase in a much greater proportion on account of the uninterrupted facilities for crossing the river that will then exist.

The average annual increase of the population in St Louis from 1835 to 1860, a period of twenty-five years, was about 12½ per cent., and the business has fully kept pace with the population, and at the present time is variously estimated at from 225,000 to 250,000. These facts give you some data from which you can estimate the amount of traffic that may be expected to find its way across the bridge.

T. B. BLACKSTONE,
A. ANDERSON,
T. McKISSOCK,
CHAS. L. TUCKER, } *Committee.*

REPORT

OF THE

BOARD OF CIVIL ENGINEERS,

CONVENED AT ST. LOUIS, IN AUGUST, 1867,

TO CONSIDER THE SUBJECT OF THE CONSTRUCTION OF A

RAIL AND HIGHWAY BRIDGE

ACROSS THE MISSISSIPPI RIVER AT ST. LOUIS.

GENERAL REPORT.

If a proposition to build a Bridge of two thousand feet in length, at an elevation of eighty-five feet above the water, with piers placed where an unstable sand of one hundred feet in depth rested upon the rock, over which flowed one of the mightiest rivers in the world, with a volume increased ten-fold in freshets, had been made a half century ago, it would have appalled the boldest men of the profession.

At the present day the engineer has the command of materials of such increased strength and improved forms, and the aid of mechanism of such power and facilities, that it is difficult to present to him a problem involving impossibilities.

The modern achievements of engineering are evidences of the astonishing march of progress in that profession, which fully keeps pace with the other professions. Bridges like the Britannia, Victoria, Niagara and Susquehanna, a steamship of over twenty thousand tons, a Thames and Chicago tunnel, and the Atlantic telegraph, are the striking types of this progress; while the huge castings of a hundred tons in iron and twenty in steel, and the forging of iron plates and beams of equal weight, the conversion of the rude pigs of iron into pure steel in twenty minutes, developing a heat of ten thousand degrees, without fuel or furnace, yield their tribute to the demand of the engineer.

But there is danger that, under the incentives of these wonderful achievements, the engineer may be led either to attempt impossibilities, or, what is more likely, to venture too far in an untried field of labor, and he would fail in his duty, and in a proper comprehension of his mission, if he allows himself to project plans merely for his own personal eclat or aggrandize ment, or does not confine himself to the most safe, practicable and reasonable methods of accomplishing the results which are desired.

In a Convention like that which has been assembled, the eccentricities of even the greatest minds would have been brought down to the consideration of the subject in its most practical form, and the comparison of opinions, and the necessity of defending them before such astute judges, would have restrained all tendency towards erratic but brilliant ideas. This consideration will have its due weight with capitalists, who are also to perform their important part in the construction of the bridge.

The appreciation of their professional responsibility has led the members of the Convention to give to the subject their most careful consideration, and the reports of the committees will show with what care and attention every question involved was discussed, and how wide a range of practical experience was brought to bear upon them; while the unanimity which characterized their general conclusions shows, beyond all reasonable doubt, that a bridge of the character designated can be constructed with the pier foundations of ample sustaining power, placed below any future action of the currents of the river, with piers of such stability as to resist the impact of the heaviest masses of ice, drift or vessels, and with a superstructure of nearly imperishable materials, and of ample, even surplus strength, when loaded with a dense crowd of people, and, at the same time, with the heaviest railway trains that can be made up; that such a bridge can be so placed as to conveniently accommodate the traffic over it by railways, road vehicles and pedestrians, and at the same time present no material obstruction to the commerce of the river and the port of St. Louis; that such a bridge can be constructed at a comparatively moderate expense, and, it may be added, with a certainty of a handsome return on the capital required.

It is not improper to remark in this connection that the subjects which have been under consideration were some time ago presented individually to many of the members of the Convention, so that when they met they brought to the examination of the various questions the results of their previous labors and thoughts on this special subject.

The reports of the several committees are so comprehensive as to leave for a general report but little more than the duty of prefacing them, and presenting for the use of the casual reader a simple resumé of the points discussed and the conclusions arrived at.

It is impossible, however, to curtail these committee reports without omitting matters material to a proper investigation of the question, and they are therefore herein copied *in extenso*, and the attention of those interested called to their particular examination.

The conjunction of the converging railroad lines from the Atlantic and interior at the same place where the changed character of the upper and lower river navigation requires a transhipment of the water-borne traffic, designates this as one of the principal places on the Mississippi where the land lines demand a crossing, and where it can be made with the least impediment to the navigation. The federal law which authorizes the construction of the bridge at St. Louis requires it to be placed with a clear height of eighty-four feet above the level of low water, and with either one span of five hundred feet clear opening over the main channel, or two spans each of three hundred and fifty feet, and forbids the use of either a draw or suspension bridge. These legal requirements limited the questions to be considered by the Board to the alternative of one very long span, or two shorter ones, across the main channel, and still shorter spans over the remainder of the channel, and to a trussed, arched or tubular superstructure.

The Joint Committee on the Regimen of the River, on the Foundations and Piers, and on the Superstructure, discussed the alternative proviso of the law in regard to the length of the spans across the main channel, and unanimously agreed that it was inadvisable to adopt the span of five hundred feet clear opening, on account of the difficulty of procuring suitable materials of the proper form, size and workmanship required to meet the extraordinary strains to which some of the members of the truss would be subjected; the increased hazard of its construction and maintenance; the large additional cost of the whole structure by the use of the long span, and because the necessities of this case do not require the use of one of such great length, for which there is no engineering precedent.

The Joint Committee, therefore, adopted the alternative of two spans of three hundred and fifty feet clear width over the main channel, and spans of two hundred and sixty-four feet over the remainder. The Board entirely concurred in the conclusion of the Joint Committee.

The report of the Committee on Regimen of the River and the Character of its Bottom, shows that at this place it is about fifteen hundred feet wide at low water, with a channel of about twenty feet depth on the west side, and a changeable bar in the middle, and that the river is subject to annual floods of thirty-six feet increased height in the early summer, and some years of a little greater height. The velocity of the current in these high floods is about 8½ miles per hour, at which time they bring down large quantities of drift-wood and trees.

The ice seldom passes out of the river when it is at a higher stage than ten feet above low water, and then, sometimes, in masses of 500,000 square feet, and a foot or more in thickness, and a velocity of two miles per hour. The ice sometimes grounds and gorges upon the bar to a depth of ten or twelve feet, and then extends back for several miles, and produces a sudden rise of eight feet of water in a few hours.

The bar in the middle of the river changes in height and extent with each flood, and is at its maximum after a flood of long duration and rapid decline from the highly turbid waters of the Missouri river, and is at its minimum after a flood, with a gradual decline from the clearer waters of the Upper Mississippi. The bed of the river sometimes changes by these floods ten or twelve feet in depth, but in no case does the scour extend to a greater depth than thirty feet below low water.

The borings made at this and other places on the river show a general uniformity in the character of the deposit above the rock, and similar to that which is now being annually made; but the lower and older portion of the deposit seems to have passed through an indurating process, resulting from pressure and the destruction of the vegetable matter during the long periods that it was undisturbed.

The material now brought down by the floods is coarse, silicious sand, and a slime of calcareous and aluminous matter mixed with vegetable mould. The coarser portions are deposited in the main channel, the finer ones on the bars, and the vegetable matter chiefly on the low grounds, and in the abandoned channels.

The material passed through by the borings was very compact, and the rock was reached at a depth of 23 feet below low water, near the west shore; at 500 feet further it was 64 feet deep, and at 500 feet still further east it was 90 feet below low water to the top of the rock. The rock itself is evidently the same stratified limestone which was developed in the two artesian wells sunk near by.

With the full and intelligent report from which the above points have been abstracted, before them, the Committee on Foundations and Piers proceeded to discuss that important branch of the subject, and arrived at the conclusion—"That it is both safe and practicable to construct a bridge at St. Louis with piers placed upon unyielding foundations upon either of the three following plans, viz:

"1. On hollow cast iron piles from four to eight feet diameter, driven by the pneumatic process purely, or by the use of the syphon pump, either to the rock, or by an expanded base placed far below the scour of the stream.

"2. By extending the piers of stone to the depth of the scour, and by means of iron caissons, similar to those used on the Susquehanna bridge, and the foundations resting on either wooden or small iron pneumatic piles; or

"3. By extending the piers, as before stated, by means of a combination of the inverted and direct iron or wooden caissons, the inverted caisson to be filled with masonry by the pneumatic process, and the direct one in the ordinary way; and, also, that the piers might be made either of solid or galleried masonry, or that the pneumatic piles might be extended to the height of the bridge seat as columns of support, and substitutes for stone masonry."

It is not necessary at this time to determine which of these plans will be best suited to the conditions of the case; but for the purpose of ascertaining a sum which would be ample to cover any possible expenditure for this portion of the structure, the plan of solid stone piers resting on a foundation of iron pneumatic piles of 8 feet in diameter driven to the rock for the two channel piers, and to a depth of 70 feet below low water for the piers for the smaller spans, and filled with cemented masonry, has been estimated upon.

In the former, the piles will be firmly bedded in the rock, and may be treated as columns of support, which shows them to be of excessive strength, and in the latter case treated as piles they will have a large excess of sustaining power. A description of these piles, and the method of driving and securing them, will be found in the minutes of the committee appended to this report.

The committee proposed that the piers should be galleried to reduce the unnecessary weight upon the foundations, but their estimates for masonry and foundations are based upon solid walls. The piers are arranged with ample stability to resist the impact or pressure of the great fields of ice, or floating drift, or vessels. The shore piers present no unusual difficulties of execution.

The Chief Engineer of the bridge estimates the cost of the foundations, piers and masonry at $2,541,007; and the committee examined those estimates sufficiently to satisfy themselves that that sum was ample.

The Committee on Superstructure has given that subject great attention and study; and, when in joint committee, furnished the data by means of which the strains upon the different members of the bridge trusses were ascertained, and also the relative costs of spans of different length. The conclusions of the Joint Committee on the subject have been already stated, and they also recommended that the western pier should be placed on the line of low water on the levee; and the eastern pier should be placed in the same position on that side of the river, with four intermediate river piers, and two abutments placed so as to bridge over the levees on each side of the river.

This arrangement gives the following spans for the bridge:

Spanning the St. Louis levee..................................	264	feet.
Two spans of 368 feet each over the main channel....	736	"
Four spans of 264 feet each..................................	1,056	"
Spanning the East St. Louis levee..........................	160	"
Total length of the main bridge................	2,216	feet.

The entire length of the bridge superstructure is 5,170 feet, and of the approaches 3,555 feet, making a total of 8,725 feet. The quantity of materials necessary in this work would build 10,102 feet of superstructure of the same spans, and 10,665 feet of embankment, of the same average depth, for a single track railroad, or altogether nearly four miles in length.

The committee describe two modes of the arrangement of the cross section of the bridge, one of which contemplates the use of three trusses, and the other of four trusses; and as they recommend and estimate upon the latter, that is the one which will be described.

The space between the two inner trusses is designed for the use of the railway, and will be fourteen feet in the clear.

The gauge of the track of one of the railroads on the Illinois side of the river is six feet, and the others are four feet eight and a half inches, which is also the gauge of one of the railroads on the Missouri side, and there is another gauge of five and a half feet, also on that side of the river.

These several gauges are to be accommodated by laying down four rails, of which two would be of common use for two of the gauges, and each one of the other two rails for the use of one of the other gauges.

The two spaces between the inside and outside trusses are designed for highway vehicles and ordinary traffic, and will be each seventeen feet wide in the clear, which will also be sufficient for the use of street cars. Two footways, each of eight feet in the clear, will be extended outward beyond the outer trusses, and protected by trussed railings, which will make the entire width of the superstructure seventy-five feet.

The grade of the railways will be carried level at an elevation of eighty-seven feet above low water for about five hundred feet on the west side of the river, and also over the two long spans over the main channel, and from thence will descend eastward at the rate of one hundred and twenty feet to the mile to the eastern end of the main bridge, and also to the end of the eastern embankment, where it meets the grade of the other railways.

From the western point above stated, the grade of the railways will be extended, by a series of small arches and colonnades, westward on a slightly ascending grade, at a proper elevation to cross all of the streets, for a distance of two thousand feet, where it meets the grade of Broadway in St. Louis, and terminates the structure in that direction.

From the same point the two highway passages and footwalks of the bridge will be extended westward on an independent structure from that for the railway, with a descent of ten feet in a distance of three hundred feet, when it will meet the grade of Second street.

At the east end of the bridge the two highway passages and footwalks will be extended eastward down the gentle slope of the embankment for a distance of six hundred feet to the level of the island. The two piers which are placed at the top of the levees on the opposite sides of the river, will each be perforated with a stairway, by means of which pedestrians can reach the footwalks of the main bridge from the levee.

The committee discussed several plans of bridge trusses, and found that the one presented by its chairman met all of the requirements of the case, giving ample strength to carry its own weight and that of a dense crowd of people upon the highway passages and the sidewalks, and, also at the same time, the heaviest possible railway train, with an amount of metal arranged in the most judicious manner, so as to introduce no unnecessary weight, and hence the least expensive plan, consistent with ample strength, that the case admitted.

The trusses will be formed of wrought and cast iron and steel. From the difficulty of procuring cast steel of the form and dimensions desired, cast iron will be used for the members which are wholly under the strain of compression; and for those which are under the strain of tension, wrought iron and steel will be used. Those of a great ratio of length to diameter, and subject to flexure, may be of cast or wrought iron or steel.

The cast iron will be of the best quality of metal—similar to that known in the trade as "gun metal." The best description of wrought iron and steel will be required.

The top of the truss will be of cast iron, the chord and tie braces of steel, and the posts of either cast or wrought iron or steel. The lateral braces will be of round wrought iron rods. The floor beams of solid rolled iron "Phœnix beams." The top struts will be of solid rolled iron "deck beams."

The flooring will be composed of longitudinal wooden stringers, covered for the roadway with two courses of plank, and for the footwalk one course. On the outer extremity of the footwalk will be placed an ornamental trussed iron railing.

The carriage ways will be provided with iron plate trams, and rails to accommodate the street cars, and will be screened from the railway passage by close, light wooden partitions.

All of the trusses will be made similar for the sake of symmetry, and the sidewalks, of ample width, will, when loaded, secure the equilibrium of the strains upon them all.

The elaborate diagrams of the strains upon each member of the several trusses proposed, and the formula used in calculating them, are given in the report of the committee.

That committee also carefully examined the detailed estimates of the cost of the superstructure, approaches, and six thousand feet of railway, amounting to $3,638,920, and covering the complete cost of the bridge except that portion which was embraced in the report of the Committee on Foundations and Piers, and the cost of the land and other damages. The Board has been furnished with a detailed estimate of the cost of the land and land damages amounting to the sum of $386,000. This estimate has been made by a gentleman well acquainted with the value of property in this place, and is no doubt substantially correct.

The Board is of the opinion that the construction of the bridge will greatly enhance the value of the adjacent property, and probably to such an extent that the surplus property embraced in this schedule, not actually required wholly for future use, will sell or lease for a sum nearly as great as any present reasonable assessment of the damages; but desirous to provide an estimate ample to meet any possible contingency, they have added the whole cost of the land to such estimate.

By adding together the reported estimates of the foundations, piers, superstructure and approaches, as stated by these two committees, and the cost of land and damages, the whole expenditure required for the work amounts to $6,564,000, which, in the judgment of this Board, is ample to cover all reasonable contingencies.

The Committee on the River Commerce, and its Navigation, have presented the whole subject so concisely that it is impossible to condense it further, and it is therefore introduced in this place.

The undersigned, a committee appointed by you to report on the "Commerce of the River, and its Navigation," beg leave to state that they have divided the subject into three different heads, as follows:

1st. The probable effect of a bridge at this particular point on the commerce of the river.

2d. Whether the bridge is adapted to the accommodation of the commercial marine.

3d. The statistics of the river trade.

Earnestly desiring to avoid a leaning towards either the one or the other of the generally conceived rival interests of river or rail, we shall proceed to briefly discuss the foregoing points.

Looking at the question of river navigation in a broad and progressive way, we are of the opinion that the time is approaching when the vast inland oceans and rivers which form so marked a feature in our western topography, will become the grand freight lines of the continent, leaving the railways to absorb the passenger and light freight traffic. With a settled state of affairs, the demand for rapid transportation of bulky merchandise will be done away with, and cheap freights by water will again assume the supremacy.

Assuming that this hypothesis is true, it is probable that the largest class of boats, arranged to accommodate both passengers and freight, will give place to a smaller, but more powerful class of steamers, adapted exclusively to freight traffic, in connection with barges.

The simultaneous agitation of twelve or fourteen projects for bridging the Mississippi river at as many different points, must necessarily give an impetus to this change.

In times gone by, before lines of railway radiated in every direction, making a rapid and sure conveyance to all parts of the country, it might have been urged with much force, that everything which tended to retard the river navigation, was a matter of public importance, and to be protested against. But now the case is entirely different; we no longer look to steamers as a means of passenger conveyance; as a general thing, even pleasure travel usually takes takes the mode of quickest transit from point to point.

Time is the great element which governs all our actions, and the want of it is such a peculiarly American characteristic, that the man who should propose a business trip to St. Paul, Cincinnati or New Orleans by water, would be considered a little short of insane.

One of the immediate and principal effects of bridging the Mississippi at this point, is thought to be the establishment of a line of demarkation between the upper and lower river trades. It is even now proposed to build a series of floating grain elevators along the northern part of the levee, which would of course tend directly to bring about this change. A system of lighterage and towage will then be established, so that steamers from the upper rivers with cargoes of grain, provisions, or other produce destined for southern ports, will discharge into barges or lighters, and thus avoid the necessity of passing under the bridge at all. In fact, many of the best informed steamboatmen say that it is their opinion that boats plying on the upper rivers will have no occasion to go below the bridge, and when once above it, will remain there the balance of their days.

As the class of steamboats adapted to the lower river are quite different from those on the upper rivers, we think this result a natural sequence, and, from the nature of things, very likely to follow. This would do away with the necessity of constantly passing the bridge, and hence remove a great objection generally urged against the erection of similar structures in navigable waters; but we venture to say that the pilot who could not see so plain a monument as a pier eighty-five feet high, and 12 to 18 feet wide at the smallest point, would hardly be able to get a license to navigate rivers, where myriads of snags rear their pointed crests, for a distance of three thousand miles at a stretch.

We propose, however, to show that the bridge is well adapted to the wants of the river marine.

Let us take the dimensions of some of the largest of the various classes of boats plying on the river.

The Northern Line Packet Company report that the largest of their boats, the Dubuque, measures as follows:

	Feet.
Length over all	235
Breadth of beam—over all	61
Height to top of pilot house (about)	45
" " chimneys "	70

The Keokuk Packet Company report that the Andy Johnson measures as follows:

	Feet.
Length over all	251
Breadth of beam—over all	72
Height to top of chimneys	70

The boats plying the Missouri and Illinois are not up to the foregoing dimensions.

The Memphis Packet Company say that the Marble City measures as follows:

	Feet.
Length over all	270
Breadth of beam—over all	74
Height to top of pilot house	63
" " chimneys	83

And the Atlantic and Mississippi Steamship Company report the dimensions of the Ruth to be:

	Feet.
Length over all (about)	312
Breadth of beam—over all (about)	85
Height to top of chimneys "	107½

The Great Republic, the largest steamer afloat on the Western rivers, measures:

	Feet.
Length over all	336
Breadth of beam	96
Height to top of chimneys (about)	105

The low water stage of the river usually exists from six to eight months of the year, during which time the level of the river would not be far from 80 feet below the lower chord of the bridge, as established by law. At the ordinary summer stage, as at present, there would be about 70 feet; while at the highest water level known, that is to say the flood of 1844, there would be 42½ feet. The principal spans, as determined by the law of Congress, are established at either 500 feet or 350 feet: now, a comparison of the foregoing data with these lengths of span, shows that the largest boat on the river would not occupy one quarter of the width of even the smallest span allowed by law, or with a tow of barges, less than one half the width.

We think that there can hardly be a doubt in the mind of any intelligent man but that the span of 350 feet is abundantly large to enable a free and unrestricted passage at all times.

With regard to the statistics of the river trade, the interval between the close of the war and the present time has been almost too short for commerce to regain its normal condition; but so far as we have been able to examine, it will serve to give an idea of the immense trade centering in our great city by means of steamers and barges. The arrivals and departures for 1866 were 7,162 steamers and barges, of which 3,546 were due to the upper rivers, or, an average of one-half for both years were from the North. These arrivals and departures taking place over a term of ten months of open river, and deducting the Sundays as days of rest for steamers while in port, would give, for say 250 days, an average arrival and departure of 28 steamers, 14 of which ply in the trade of the Missouri, Upper Mississippi and its tributaries. Allowing that each boat timed its arrival for the day, as is usually the case, there would be about one boat per hour passing through or under any bridge located at this point. But the records of arrivals and departures show that during the spring and fall months the movement of steamers is increased very considerably, so that at the busiest season, not far from one steamer per half hour would on an average pass over the site of the proposed bridge.

The registered tonnage of steamers running on the Upper Mississippi, Missouri, Illinois, and their tributaries, was stated to be on the 1st July, 1866, as follows:

RIVERS.	STEAM-BOATS.	BARG'S	TOTAL.	REGIST'D TONS.	TONS CAPACITY.	VALUATION.
Up'r Mississippi	44	67	111	16,560	30,685	$1,625,000
Illinois	16	25	41	5,535	10,355	488,000
Missouri	71	...	71	23,232	38,525	2,545,000
	131	92	223	45,327	79,565	$4,658,000
L'wr Mississippi	134	30	264	61,299	106,450	$5,718,000

Or, in short, $\frac{42}{100}$ of the registered tonnage, or $\frac{44}{100}$ of the entire value of the river marine of this port is engaged in transporting those freights which are destined to pass through the spans of the proposed bridge.

A retrospective glance over a term of years might give a better idea of the importance of our river interests, but we believe that what data we have furnished will show the necessity of harmonizing the details of the bridge with the far-reaching requirements of the river navigation.

In conclusion, the committee would state that, having read Mr. S. S. Post's very able and comprehensive manuscript, entitled the "City of St. Louis," would respectfully request that the same may be embodied with the foregoing, either as a portion of the original report, or as an appendix thereto, believing, as they do, that it will serve to give a more perfect idea of the wants and resources of this great commercial metropolis, than our hasty report possibly can.

Respectfully submitted on behalf of the committee.

Fred'k A. Churchill.

St. Louis, August 26, 1867.

Mr. Post's paper, headed "St. Louis," which the committee requested to be connected with their report, will be found among the reports of the committees. It shows the progressive increase of the population and business of the city, and the prospective increase based upon that of the past. As the paper also treats of the same subject as that referred to the Committee on the Commerce crossing the Bridge, the abstract of the two will be presented together.

The tonnage brought to the river opposite St. Louis by the existing Illinois railroads is over a million of tons per annum, of which nearly one-half is the ordinary products of the country, and the remainder in coal. The Illinois railroads also bring annually nearly half a million of passengers.

The railroads of Missouri already bring in to St. Louis a quantity of freight and passengers nearly as great as those of Illinois, and these roads are now being extended with a rapidity almost marvellous. One railroad to the north will soon drain the rich Des Moines Valley, even into the State of Minnesota, and the same road, by its tap of the St. Joseph and Leavenworth branches, already brings a vast eastward bound business to St. Louis. The Pacific railroad and its namesake. now being rapidly extended westward, will, in another year, reach the rich gold regions of Colorado, while the Southwestern and Iron Mountain railroads, already far into the interior, are being rapidly extended.

The trade already existing is sufficient to warrant the construction of such a bridge as the one designed, and with the certainty of an enormous increase of traffic, it leaves no reasonable doubt in the mind that the bridge will receive a business and a revenue which will warrant the expenditure for its construction.

In bringing their labors to a conclusion, the Board take the opportunity of expressing their thanks to the officers of the Bridge Company and of the several Railroad Companies, and also to the gentlemen of the vicinity for many courtesies extended to the members, and for very valuable local information which has facilitated their examinations.

It is also the unanimous expression of the members of the Board that they have all individually received most valuable information by the mutual interchange of opinions, and by the discussion of some of the most important and interesting problems in engineering which the practical operations previously carried on by the members have enabled them to furnish.

It is also particularly gratifying that all of the members have been so frank in furnishing their respective quotas of this information, and the harmony and genial feeling displayed results in separating with an increased devotion to the profession, and of their mutual respect for each other.

(Signed,)

WM. J. McALPINE, Civil Engineer, *N. Y.*
GEO. A. PARKER, " " *Pa.*
E. S. CHESBROUGH, " " *Ill.*
W. S. SMITH, " " *Mich.*

L. J. FLEMING,	Civil	Engineer,	*Ala.*
A. ANDERSON,	"	"	*Kansas.*
C. L. McALPINE,	"	"	*Mass.*
T. J. HOMER,	"	"	*Mo.*
J. B. MOULTON,	"	"	*Mo.*
T. B. BLACKSTONE,	"	"	*Ill.*
T. McKISSOCK,	"	"	*Mo.*
R. M. SHOEMAKER,	"	"	*Ohio.*
O. CHANUTE,	"	"	*Kansas.*
F. A. CHURCHILL,	"	"	*Mo.*
S. S. POST,	"	"	*N. J.*
R. B. MASON,	"	"	*Ill.*
JULIUS W. ADAMS,	"	"	*N. Y.*
W. E. MERRILL,	Brevet-Col. U. S. Engineers.		
WM. E. WORTHEN,	Civil	Engineer,	*N. Y.*
JOHN E. HENRY,	"	"	*Iowa.*
S. F. JOHNSON,	"	"	*R. I.*
L. H. CLARK,	"	"	*Ill.*
JAS. H. MORLEY,	"	"	*Mo.*
E. H. JOHNSON,	"	"	*Ill.*
W. W. EVANS,	"	"	*N. Y.*
F. HUBBARD,	"	"	*N. Y.*
D. C. JENNE,	"	"	*N. Y.*
IRA SPAULDING,	"	"	*N. Y.*

EXTRACTS FROM THE MANUSCRIPT

TO WHICH REFERENCE IS MADE BY THE

COMMITTEE ON RIVER AND ITS NAVIGATION.

The city of St. Louis, the great inland metropolis of America, is admirably situated on the western bank of the Mississippi river, in north latitude 38° 37½′, and longitude 13° 13¾′ west from Washington, 400 feet above the level of the ocean, and 60 feet above the river. It has a harbor which can accommodate many hundreds of steamboats of the largest class; and the surrounding country is fertile, well cultivated, and populous. The area of the city is about 36 square miles, and is filling up with unexampled rapidity.

St. Louis was founded in 1764 by the French from Canada as a trading post with the Indians, but during the French and Spanish possession of it, remained an inconsiderable village. In 1799, it contained a population of 925. In 1828, the population was 5,000, an average annual increase of about 6 per cent. In 1850, the population was 74,439, an average annual increase of 13 per cent. since 1828. In 1860, the population was 160,773, an average annual increase since 1860 of 8 per cent. In 1866, the population was 204,327, an average annual increase of only $4\frac{1}{10}$ per cent. since 1860. During a greater portion of this last period the commercial prosperity of this city suffered severely from the blockade of the Mississippi, and other effects of the civil war. The prostration of business was general and disastrous. Property in real estate fell to about half its former value. In 1860, the real estate in St. Louis was assessed at $73,765,670. In 1865, after the close of the war, the real estate was assessed but $73,960,700, showing a gain in the valuation of only $195,030 in five years. The assessed value of the real estate in 1866 was $81,961,610, a gain of $8,000,910 in one year. The real and personal property was assessed in 1865 at $100,000,000; in 1866, at $126,877,000. Increase in one year, $26,877,000. From this time forward, for at least many years, it is probable that St. Louis will increase both in population and wealth as rapidly as it has done in any period of its former history. From 1835 to 1860, an unbroken term of twenty-five years, the population has gone up from 8,316 to 160,673, an average annual increase of $12\frac{577}{1000}$ per cent. An increase of $12\frac{1}{2}$ per cent. per annum adds $\frac{1}{8}$ to the population every year. At this rate it will be—

In 1866	204,327	In 1871	412,655
" 1867	229,868	" 1872	464,237
" 1868	258,600	" 1873	522,267
" 1869	290,925	" 1874	587,550
" 1870	366,795	" 1875	660,869

* * * * * * * * *

In 1854 the first portion of any railroad from St. Louis—the Pacific of Missouri—was opened to Franklin, now the town of Pacific, 38 miles from the city. Previous to this date all the carrying trade of St. Louis, or nearly all, was effected by means of steamboats. The tonnage of steamboats and barges plying between St. Louis and other ports on the Mississippi, Missouri, Illinois, Cumberland, Tennessee, Arkansas and White rivers, July 1, 1866, was 265 steamers and 122 barges, altogether registered at 106,626 tons, and valued at $10,376,000. A great number of canal boats and barges arrive by the Illinois and Upper Mississippi rivers, not registered at St. Louis, and not included in the tonnage.

The railroads centering at St. Louis at this time are the Pacific, the North Missouri, the St. Louis and Iron Mountain, the Ohio and Mississippi, the Chicago, Alton and St. Louis, and the St. Louis, Alton and Terre Haute Railroads.

To show that the trade of St. Louis has fully kept pace with the population, the receipts of breadstuffs for the years 1860 and 1866 are given:

FLOUR IN BARRELS.

1860	443,196	1866	1,208,726

Increase per annum, $18\frac{2}{10}$ per cent.

GRAIN IN BUSHELS.

1860.		1866.	
Wheat	2,654,738	Wheat	4,410,305
Corn	4,249,782	Corn	7,233,671
Oats	1,832,634	Oats	3,567,000
Rye	159,974	Rye	375,417
Barley	339,974	Barley	548,796
Total	9,237,102	Total	16,135,189

Average annual increase of $9\frac{3}{4}$ per cent.

Of this kind of produce, steamers and barges have had the greater share, and probably will have for many years to come. A very fair proportion of this carrying trade, however, is already being done by the railroads before mentioned, and will rapidly increase as their lines are extended.

The receipts and imports at St. Louis of flour and grain, by rail, in 1865 and in 1866, were as follows, in lbs.:

BY THE PACIFIC RAILROAD.

	Receipts. 1865.	1866.		*Exports.* 1865.	1866.
Flour	2,970,400	2,480,000	Flour	....	7,314,000
Wheat	5,490,060	12,926,240	Wheat	....	493,440
Corn	1,182,944	9,962,960	Corn	....	516,624
Oats	227,446	282,260	Oats	....	298,760
Rye	....	45,584	Rye	....	124,376
Barley	3,338,974	4,572,048	Barley	....	56,489
Total	13,209,824	30,269,092	Total	....	8,803,689

BY THE ST. LOUIS AND IRON MOUNTAIN RAILROAD.

	Receipts. 1865.	1866.	*Exports.* 1865.	1866.
Flour	90,100	404,200		
Wheat	245,880	597,480		
Corn	55,324	89,154		
Oats	35,492	16,112		
Rye	....	....		
Barley	11,501	71,562		
Total	438,297	1,178,508		

BY THE NORTH MISSOURI RAILROAD.

	Receipts. 1865.	1866.		*Exports.* 1865.	1866.
Flour	494,400	1,356 200	Flour	....	5,035,800
Wheat	9,989,520	10,333,926	Wheat	....	216,700
Corn	320,320	4,675,456	Corn	....	....
Oats	1,171,692	1,537,060	Oats	....	675,960
Rye	101,808	19,152	Rye	....	43,376
Barley	294,690	271,920	Barley	....	257,224
Total	12,372,430	18,193,714	Total	....	6,229,060

BY THE OHIO AND MISSISSIPPI RAILROAD.

Receipts.	1865.	1866.	Exports.	1865.	1866.
Flour	28,672,000	28,250,300	Flour	11,382,000	36,326,000
Wheat	2,544,440	5,677,920	Wheat	....	9,367,560
Corn	1,396,866	11,861,024	Corn	....	....
Oats	1,214,024	5,425,980	Oats	....	291,066
Rye	135,076	137,200	Rye	549,312	2,173,366
Barley	494,625	118,032	Barley	74,166	1,266,384
Total	34,467,031	51,470,456	Total	11,915,478	49,424,376

BY THE CHICAGO, ALTON AND ST. LOUIS RAILROAD.

Receipts.	1865.	1866.	Exports.	1865.	1866.
Flour	13,765,200	19,607,800	Flour	7,057,200	17,867,400
Wheat	2,751,548	13,503,370	Wheat	....	134,820
Corn	18,214,336	65,060,580	Corn	....	158,032
Oats	3,441,132	8,452,430	Oats	....	2,602
Rye	100,688	314,565	Rye	....	11,480
Barley	265,832	381,756	Barley	25,662	91,200
Total	38,538,736	107,320,491	Total	7,082,862	18,265,534

BY THE ST. LOUIS, ALTON AND TERRE HAUTE RAILROAD.

Receipts.	1865.	1866.	Exports.	1865.	1866.
Flour	65,126,600	64,428,800	Flour	16,970,000	43,513,200
Wheat	7,715,280	15,748,000	Wheat	2,350,200	3,111,360
Corn	15,421,504	24,732,624	Corn	7,200	2,240
Oats	5,910,190	12,923,400	Oats	6,308	122,426
Rye	114,432	372,912	Rye	....	79,128
Barley	662,388	466,560	Barley	175,686	68,204
Total	94,950,394	118,673,269	Total	19,409,394	46,896,558

RECAPITULATION.

Receipts.

	1865.	1866.
Pacific Railroad	13,209,824	30,269,092
Iron Mountain Railroad	438,297	1,178,508
North Missouri Railroad	12,372,430	18,193,714
Total Missouri Railroads	26,020,550	49,640,314

Exports.

	1865.	1866.
Pacific Railroad	....	8,803,689
Iron Mountain Railroad	....	....
North Missouri Railroad	....	6,227,060
Total Missouri Railroads	....	15,030,749

Receipts.

	1865.	1866.
Ohio and Mississippi Railroad	34,467,031	51,070,456
Chicago, Alton and St. Louis Railroad	38,538,736	107,320,491
St. Louis, Alton and Terre Haute Railroad	94,950,394	118,673,296
Total Illinois Railroads	167,795,161	277,064,243

Exports.

	1865.	1866.
Ohio and Mississippi Railroad	....	49,424,376
Chicago, Alton and St. Louis Railroad	....	18,265,534
St. Louis, Alton and Terre Haute Railroad	....	46,896,558
Total Illinois Railroads	....	114,586,468

	1865.	1866.
Grand Total Receipts	193,976,712	326,705,557
" " Exports	....	129,617,217

The receipts by Railroad in 1866 were therefore—

Flour	726,246	barrels,	or	60	per cent.	of all.
Wheat	979,782	bushels	"	22	"	"
Corn	2,078,246	"	"	29	"	"
Oats	818,207	"	"	23	"	"
Rye	15,900	"	"	4	"	"
Barley	122,539	"	"	22	"	"

There was received by wagons at St. Louis in 1866—

Flour	181,890	barrels,	or	15	per cent.	of total	receipts.
Wheat	200,000	bushels	"	$4\frac{1}{2}$	"	"	"
Corn	300,000	"	"	$4\frac{1}{8}$	"	"	"
Oats	100,000	"	"	$2\frac{8}{10}$	"	"	"

The foregoing statements do not include the 818,300 bbls. of flour which were manufactured in the city of St. Louis in 1866.

The *receipts* of flour and grain at St. Louis from all the railroads in 1866, were two and a quarter times greater than in 1865.

The exports, by rail, of breadstuffs in 1865, not being easily ascertained, no comparisons are here made, but the ratio will probably not differ much from that of the receipts for the two years as above given.

* * * * * * *

The receipts and exports at St. Louis by the Illinois railroads in 1866, of all kinds of freight, exclusive of coal, were as follows:

	Receipts.	*Exports.*
Chicago, Alton and St. Louis Railroad........	131,713 tons.	24,951 tons.
Ohio and Mississippi Railroad....................	94,438 "	61,013 "
St. Louis, Alton and Terre Haute Railroad,	90,649 "	67,739 "
Total except coal..................................	316,900 tons.	153,703 tons.

Making the aggregate in both directions 470,503 tons transported to and from the cars across the river on boats.

The coal brought to the river by the Illinois railroads is 544,500 tons, most of which goes over to the St. Louis side.

Large quantities of grain, and of the many other agricultural products of Illinois, crowd the ferry boats that are plying between St. Louis and the opposite shore during the day.

* * * * * * *

The river at St. Louis is often closed by ice, so that ferry boats cannot run. Some years this happens during the greater part of the winter. At times the condition of the ice is such as to preclude crossing there in any manner for several successive days. The ferry boat, even when the river is clear of ice, seldom runs between sunset and sunrise, and belated teams and travelers from the east are forced to remain on the Illinois shore until the boats resume their trips in the morning. At low water, access to the boats by teams is extremely difficult and hazardous, in consequence of the steepness and irregularity of the banks of the river on both sides, and the changing sands on the Illinois shore particularly.

* * * * * * *

On the 20th of February, 1867, the Illinois and St. Louis Bridge Company was regularly incorporated in Missouri by filing articles of association in the office of the Secretary of State, in accordance with the general laws, approved March 19, 1866, for the formation of Bridge Companies in this State.

On the 21st of February, 1867, a special charter from Illinois to the same Company, exceedingly liberal in its provisions, was approved by the Governor of that State; and on the 1st of March,

1867, the necessary subscription to the stock having been made, the Company was fully organized by the election of a Board of Directors.

Since March 1st, the Company has exercised the utmost diligence in making the necessary surveys, procuring the most reliable statistics possible, and making estimates on various plans of construction.

The Illinois and St. Louis Bridge Company have a perpetual charter from the State of Illinois, with powers of consolidating with any other Bridge Company, for the purpose of maintaining a toll bridge from any point or place on the Mississippi river opposite the city of St. Louis, and has the *exclusive right for twenty-five years* of constructing such bridge.

* * * * * * *

It has been observed that 470,500 tons of freight, besides coal, was transported in 1866 across the river to and from the Illinois railroads. Assuming that this business crossing the river shall increase in the same ratio as the increase of the population and business has been for the 25 years, already shown—and it certainly will increase in a much higher ratio when the bridge shall be completed—then the tonnage for the year 1871, should the bridge not be completed before that time, will be 848,036 tons. The coal delivered at the river from Illinois, at the same ratio of increase, will be 978,442 tons in 1871.

Passengers to and from St. Louis by the Illinois railroads in 1866 were 479,200. Allowing the same rate of increase as for the population of St. Louis for the 25 years, and this number of railroad passengers will be increased to 863,509 in 1871.

The whole population of East St. Louis will be likely to cross the bridge many times a year, and it is undoubtedly safe to assume that the foot travel will be fully equal to that of each person in St. Louis passing both ways five times a year, which, in 1871, would be 4,126,550 passages.

The average number of teams of various kinds (other than the Transfer Company's teams and coal teams which cross the ferry daily) is not less than one thousand. Calling these teams 300,000 per annum at the present time, and supposing them to increase as the population, they will be 540,607 in 1871. Great numbers of cattle, hogs, horses, mules, &c., in droves, also cross the river at St. Louis; but these will probably be merged in the railroad traffic in future years.

7

No allowance is made above for the increased traffic which the building of the bridge would occasion between the city of St. Louis and the great manufacturing towns which will spring up at East St. Louis, Illinoistown and vicinity, on the completion of the bridge. Grain elevators, lumber yards and various other branches of business seeking locations on the river shore, will find accommodations on the Illinois as well as the Missouri bank of the Mississippi.

If the bridge shall be completed on or before January 1st, 1871, the receipts for the year 1871 may be safely estimated as follows:

850,000 tons of freight, at 75 cents	$637,500
978,442 tons of coal, at 50 cents	489,221
863,000 railroad passengers, at 25 cents	215,750
4,125,000 foot passengers, at 5 cents	206,250
540,000 teams, at 30 cents	162,000
Cattle, hogs, horses, mules, &c., as freight	100,000
Total	$1,810,721

These rates are very low, whether compared with the present cost of ferriage at St. Louis, or with the tolls charged at other bridges over the Mississippi river.

The cost of maintenance and attendance of this bridge will be relatively very small in comparison with its receipts—say $50,000 per annum, equal to three-fourths of one per cent. of its estimated cost.

If the quantities estimated prove correct, and the rates are reduced one-half, the increase will be $905,360—$50,000=$855,360. At the rates as first given, and allowing $75,000 for cattle, &c., the traffic of 1866 would net $1,005,313—$50,000=$955,313, or 14½ per cent. on the estimated cost.

The annual saving to the people of St. Louis and the public generally in 1871, as the result of the construction of the bridge, is estimated to be—

On 850,000 tons of freight, at 45 cents	$382,500
On 978,442 tons of coal, at 50 cents	489,221
On 863,000 railroad passengers, at 25 cents	135,750
On 540,000 teams, other than transfer and coal, at 20 cents	108,000
Losses by detention	1,500,000
Total	$2,615,471

This sum for detention appears very large; but it should be remembered that coal teams make 5 or 6 trips across the ice in the winter, while they will not average more than 2½ trips on the ferry. All other business is correspondingly delayed.

Should the rates be reduced to 50 cents per ton for freight; 25 for coal; railroad passengers, 15 cents; foot passengers, 3 cents, and teams, 20 cents, the annual income from the last mentioned quantities would be $1,121,810 50, or, more than 17 per cent. of the estimated cost of the bridge; and, calling the losses by detention $1,500,000, as before, the annual saving to St. Louis and the public would be $3,321,181 50, or more than half enough to construct the bridge.

* * * * * * *

Besides the railroads centering at St. Louis, as already described, others are being extended westward, northward and southward, which soon—some of them this year to a certain extent—will contribute immensely to the trade of this city. Among them are:

* * * * * * *

The Missouri Valley Railroad (formerly the Platte Co. Railroad) extending from Leavenworth to Council Bluffs. This road is being rapidly constructed, and a portion of it north of St. Joseph is complete.

The Iowa Central Railroad Company will extend their line to Minneapolis, making a continuous and direct connection between that point and St. Louis—a distance of 575 miles—intersecting the Hannibal and St. Joseph Railroad, the Burlington and Missouri Railroad, the Des Moines Valley Railroad, the Chicago, Rock Island and Pacific Railroad, the Northwestern Railroad, the Winona and St. Peters Railroad, and several others running westward from the Mississippi, already built, or in process of construction.

* * * * * * *

The Victoria bridge, over the St. Lawrence river, at Montreal, cost over $8,000,000 in gold, at a time when labor and materials of all kinds were from 50 to 75 per cent. below the present prices in the States. The superstructure of that bridge is 6,138 feet long. It consists of a rectangular hollow tube, 16 feet wide, and from 18½ to 22 feet high, made of iron plates like boiler iron, and put together with 2½ millions of rivets. It accommodates only a single track railway, there being no carriage way or sidewalk required. The greatest depth of the water is 22 feet, and the under side of the superstructure is but 60 feet above the water. The bottom of the river is solid rock, so that no pneumatic piles were necessary.

The superstructure is divided into 25 spans, one of which is 330 feet, and the others 242 feet from centre t, centre of the piers, consequently the masonry consists of two butments and approaches, and 24 piers, containing altogether about 300,000,000 cubic feet of masonry. Of timber, there were used 2¼ millions feet, B. M., for temporary works in constructing and raising the bridge. The first stone was laid July 20, 1854, and the first passenger train crossed December 17, 1859, so that the time consumed in the actual construction of the work was 5½ years, or more.

* * * * * * *

Steam and the magnetic telegraph are rapidly producing the most extraordinary changes in the commercial world, in the systems of exchange and finance generally, but the most powerful agent is the telegraph.

We may not be able to foresee exactly what may result in the future, but so far as we have seen, it is evident that we are on the eve of a much greater revolution in these matters. We may be certain that the nation which occupies the most commanding portion of the globe; which has the most varied resources, and the most intelligent citizens to develop them, must be the financial centre of the world. The United States hold that position and possess these advantages; while St. Louis is geographically and commercially the centre of the United States. New York city is the metropolis; it will become more important than Venice ever was, and will shortly eclipse even London. Time is money—by means of the telegraph, and for much less per cent. than the brokerages have formerly been, a merchant in St. Louis can pay a bill in New York, San Francisco, or any other city in the United States, on the day of maturity. The same is true of most cities of Europe; and how long will it be before the same advantages extend to Asia and the whole world? We are in the centre of the world; with one hand stretched out on Europe, the other on Asia, we will control the interchange of their commerce, and the business will pass this way. St. Louis will be the great central depôt between New York and San Francisco, and these are destined to be the largest cities of this continent.

Perspective View of the Illinois & St. Louis Bridge

www.ingramcontent.com/pod-product-compliance
Lightning Source LLC
LaVergne TN
LVHW011119110826
845150LV00008B/2182
* 9 7 8 1 4 2 5 5 0 6 8 6 5 *